MIDAS MARKETING

How Midas Managers Make Markets

Midas Marketing
How Midas Managers Make Markets
www.midasnation.com

Edited by John Grooms
Cover, page design and cartoons drawn by Greg Russell

Library of Congress Cataloging-in-Publication Data

Slee, Robert T.

    Midas Marketing: how Midas Managers make markets / Rob Slee – 1st ed.
      p. cm.

      ISBN 978-0-9790478-2-4
      1. Private business-Marketing.   2. Success in business.   3. Global economy.
      I. Title

To all those chasing their absurd idea

MIDAS MARKETING

How
Midas Managers
Make Markets

Rob Slee

ABOUT THE AUTHOR

Rob is founder of MidasNation, a community that is dedicated to helping business owners increase the value of their firms (www. MidasNation.com).

Rob has published more than one hundred fifty articles on private finance topics in a variety of legal and business journals. Rob's book, *Private Capital Markets*, was published in mid-2004 by John Wiley & Sons. This book is now considered the seminal work in finance for private companies. Rob's second book, *Midas Managers*, was published in early 2007. This book was a top seller in that year.

Rob is a board member of numerous professional associations and private companies. He has owned equity positions in a variety of mid-sized private businesses. He is a Phi Beta Kappa graduate of Miami University, and received a Master's degree from the University of Chicago and an MBA from Case Western Reserve University. Rob can be reached at: r.slee@midasnation.com.

Rob is still best known as the father of Jen and Jessie Slee, his identical twin daughters.

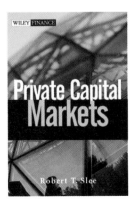 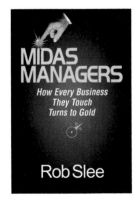

TABLE OF CONTENTS

PREFACE

It's getting easy to identify with a rat on a wheel. In this era of exponential change, most people — business owners included — are working harder than ever but aren't getting anywhere. They're behind the tidal wave of change, and it makes them anxious, exasperated, and feeling more than a little defeated. Fear not, for this book can get you back on the crest of the wave.

I'm on a mission. After successfully owning numerous businesses, and advising countless more, I have concerns about Main Street's ability to compete in a global economy. It matters: private businesses generate the majority of the U.S. economy, yet at least 80% of business owners are not currently increasing the value of their firms. I can see this because I stand outside the Matrix of denial — that self-imposed realm in which so many Americans have imprisoned themselves. These "ultimate insiders" believe that globalization is a fad; that if they continue to ignore cutting-edge technology long enough, it will just go away; and that all they have to do is hang in there and everything will be OK. Yeah, right. I've been outside the Matrix since 2002. As in the movies of the same name, it's cold outside the Matrix. We have to use our brains, our wits, and our guts out here. But at least we feel the exhilarating possibilities of the global reality. And fortunately, thousands of escapees are out here with us.

So what have we learned outside the Matrix? That we can win. Not just win, but win big. The global reality gives ... and it takes away. It especially gives to those who face it head on. Sure, it can be confusing, even overwhelming. I tell tens of thousands of business owners each year that the only thing harder than escaping the Matrix is continuing to live there.

Let me be your guide to live and prosper in this new reality. *Midas Managers* was published in 2007, and it illustrates life in the Conceptual Age. That book shows how to reconceptualize your role and business model to better compete in the global economy. When in doubt, imitate the super-successful. The stories in *Midas Managers* enable you to do that.

Midas Marketing shows you how to make markets like Midas Managers. This book empowers you to leverage your intellectual capital by more than 20:1, meaning that you can increase your output 20-fold, without adding proportionate resources. In fact, you must do this, because you are competing against companies that have already achieved this advanced level of effectiveness. By the time you read this book, most industry spaces around the globe will be dominated by handfuls of companies that are achieving better than 20:1 leverage. And they're not stopping or slowing down. It doesn't take many competitors in a supply chain with leverage like this to crowd out the non-leveraged. Welcome to the "Aggregation Age." Think of it as the "Conceptual Age" on steroids.

I've realized late in life the importance of marketing. Like many MBAs, I was taught that the road to riches lies on the finance path, with marketing providing the cake courses along the way. This type of bias likely accounts for the air of superiority emanating from Wall Street, where the smartest guys in the room all seem to wear finance MBAs from the top schools. In the last five or so years, however, I have seen the light. Maybe leaving the Matrix caused this. One major impediment has been that most marketing academics I've met aren't focused on Main Street (although they can't hold a candle to their finance brothers and sisters in this regard). But by attending my new school — Hard Knocks University — I now fully appreciate that marketing is where it's at.

As you will read, however, I've also come to realize that marketing and sales are not the same thing — not even close. Those companies that confer business titles such as "VP of Sales & Marketing" just don't get it. Because marketing sets the condition for a sale. Marketing is a strategic activity; sales is tactical. This functional difference was well-understood in ancient China. Sun Tzu, the warrior-philosopher, said: "Strategy without tactics is the slowest route to victory. Tactics without strategy is the noise before defeat." Different skill sets are required for each of these functions. Typically, the same person can't do both jobs. If the same person could perform both functions (which they can't), the title would be "VP of Marketing & Sales."

I further believe and demonstrate in these pages that most salespeople are marked for extinction. Marketing in the Aggregation Age is ending the existence of the traditional cold-calling, push-it-out-the-door salesperson. Sure, there will always be salespeople - for the one-off sale. But the one-off sale usually doesn't create value. In these pages, I clearly show that companies leveraging their intellectual capital more than 20:1 are doing it without traditional salespeople. Most managers should be thrilled with this news. They've long suspected that salespeople aren't really adding value, and that there must be a better way to generate revenues. Read on.

MARKETING TERMINOLOGY

This is probably the first marketing book you have ever read. I understand why: I was once where you are now. Most business books are written about large, public companies — the GE Way, Life at P&G, etc. — and you don't care about these companies and how they do it. Nor should you. You're smart enough to know that small private companies operate differently from their intergalactic public counterparts.

Let me begin by clarifying some marketing terminology. The following is a brief primer with everything you need to know.

1. Let's say a typically obnoxious investment banker sees a pretty woman at a party. He goes up to her and says, "I'm a fantastic kisser."

That's Direct Marketing.

2. The typical investment banker is at a party with a bunch of friends and sees a pretty woman. One of his friends (as if) goes up to her and, pointing at the banker, says, "He's a fantastic kisser."

That's Advertising.

3. The banker sees a pretty woman at a party. He goes up to her and gets her telephone number. The next day he calls and says, "Hi, I'm a fantastic kisser."

That's Telemarketing.

4. The banker sees a woman at a party; he walks up to her and pours her a drink. He then tells her about a movie she would enjoy, and says, "By the way, I'm a fantastic kisser."

That's Public Relations.

5. He's at a party and sees a pretty woman. She walks up to him and says, "I hear you're a fantastic kisser."

That's Brand Recognition.

6. He's at a party and sees a pretty woman. She fancies him, but the banker talks her into going on a date with his friend instead.

That's a Sales Rep.

7. The typical investment banker's friend and the women do not hit it off, so she calls the banker to complain about the introduction.

That's Tech Support.

8. The banker is on his way to a party when he realizes that there could be pretty women in all these houses he's passing, so he climbs onto the roof of one situated towards the center and shouts at the top of his lungs, "I'm a fantastic kisser!"

That's Junk Mail.

Now you know enough about marketing terminology to teach a course on it. Or, at the least, you should have something to talk about at future parties.

I make people in the Matrix quite nervous. They really have no point of reference in dealing with me, with their being locked in a fantasy world and all. Sometimes I do wonder if tackling the world's problems isn't best left to someone else. But now is the time for outrageous, out-there thinking and action. T. Boone Pickens is right when he says that "it's time to do something, even if it's wrong."

In times of trouble I look for guidance from the great minds in human history. Perhaps no greater thinker has existed than Einstein, and he said that, "If at first the idea is not absurd, then there is no hope for it." Let's hear it for Uncle Albert! You're probably working on your 20th absurd idea (at least) this year. This book is written for you.

INVESTMENT BANKER MAN

Why it's so hard for owners to buy
what marketing professors are selling

MIDAS MARKETING

arketing sets the condition for a sale. Midas Marketing goes farther and sets the condition for a value-added sale. Many of the most successful companies in the world rely on Midas Marketing strategies. And these practices are available to you. By the end of this book you will own the ability to make markets and dramatically increase the value of your business. Let's get started.

When performed correctly, Midas Marketing creates such a strong pull on customers that they not only buy your products and services, but they also become valuable stakeholders in your company. Moreover, companies that adopt Midas Marketing strategies eliminate all or most of their salespeople. Who needs pushy salespeople when customers are pulled through the door? Be careful, though. Don't yet act like the business owner in Chicago who called a sales meeting and announced to his 20 salespeople that their jobs would be at risk as soon as *Midas Marketing* was available. After a few minutes of total quiet, one salesman finally raised his hand and asked when the book was scheduled to be released.

Midas Marketing correctly portrays marketing as a strategic activity that sets the stage for a tactical sale. But not just any sale; rather, a sale that creates value for the firm. It turns out that not all sales are created equal. Take General Motors and Toyota, for instance. Both companies have roughly the same annual revenues, but Toyota is more valuable than GM by more than a factor of 50.

This book illustrates how Midas Managers create wealth by making markets. Midas Managers are the heroes of my prior book of the same name. These men and women consistently increase the value of their business holdings, regardless of industry conditions or economic cycles. It's more than good luck, since the same people strike gold again and again. These wealth-creators just seem to have the Midas touch.

Midas Managers are a rare breed: they account for less than 1% of all businesspeople. This, in part, explains the lack of value currently being created by private owners. Less than a quarter of private companies in the U.S. will be worth more in five years than they are today. Fortunately, we can all copy the strategies and tactics of the super-successful managers. This is especially true in marketing, as the blueprints outlined later in the book are available to all managers.

Midas Managers are also unusual people. They build substantial wealth based on market knowledge, and the ability, as legendary entrepreneur Ted Turner describes it, to see "just over the horizon." They are motivated by money, but seek to create both personal and business wealth. They focus on a few critical success factors and use straightforward metrics to measure their progress toward them. They understand the behavior and motives of players around them. They are reflective, but with enough salesmanship to get what they want. They think strategically, but act practically. They usually master only one or two wealth-creating strategies; then they look for situations where they can apply these same strategies over and over. More often than not, they are contrarians. J. Paul Getty, a Midas Manager of the first degree, famously summed up their mindset when he said that "no one can possibly achieve any real and lasting success ... by being a conformist." Finally, they use building wealth via the business as the primary scorecard. As Warren Buffett, the alpha Midas Manager of our time says, "the only thing better than making money, is making a whole lot of money."

I have now met some 200 Midas Managers. The thing that strikes me about this group is their "back of the room" persona. They do not typically flaunt their wealth (needless to say, then, Donald Trump is not a Midas Manager), and they will not enforce their considerable wills outside of their businesses unless asked to do so. Since almost all of them failed early in their business careers, they have a special relationship with failure. They understand that oblivion is just one phone call away, and sometimes the phone doesn't give you even that courtesy.

Midas Managers absolutely understand how to make markets. In a Midas-managed company, most employees have absolutely no idea what the Midas Manager does. This is because the Manager spends most of his/her time in the markets. Niche opportunities and the next big idea are out "there," not in the corner office. Because

MIDAS MOMENT

of this worldview, Midas Managers throughout history have been
early adopters of new technologies, more effective business models, and especially the changing rules of business.

BUSINESS AGES

Every so often, the rules of business change. In the past 200 years
this has occurred several times. First came the Industrial Revolu-
tion, which in the early 19th century ushered in the Industrial Age.
John Henry may have beaten the mechanical spike-driver in lore,
but machines have dominated in every other way for more than 150
years. Next came the Information Age, which began in the 1950's
with the arrival of computers and reached a climax in the 1990's
with the explosion of the Internet. Computers changed the way we
work, making complex jobs easy and enabling routine tasks to be
performed at ever-lower costs. During this Age, knowledge workers and MBAs reigned supreme.

On September 11, 2001, we entered the Conceptual Age. The
United States was thrust into a global war with terrorists. At about
the same time, China entered the World Trade Organization. The
combination of these events birthed the Conceptual Age and thrust
U.S. businesses into a global war of their own. The Conceptual Age
marks the intersection of globalization, logistics, and advanced
technology. This Age is defined by multi-dimensional thinking, and
requires business owners to conceptualize their way to success. Operational excellence is no longer enough. In the Conceptual Age, it
is merely the starting point. Machines, capital and employees are
no longer the main factors in creating business wealth. Out with the
MBAs, and in with the MODs (Masters of Design). In the Conceptual Age, the biggest constraint is the manager's ability to concep-

tualize solutions. Walt Disney would be proud: our imaginations now drive value creation.

But now as we enter the second decade of the new millennium, a new Age of business is dawning: the Aggregation Age. This Age reflects the reality that firms around the world have evolved and learned to leverage their intellectual capital in ways that were not possible just ten years ago. Firms are aggregating their industry spaces without actually owning them. Control — not own — your sphere of influence is the mantra of this Age. Because change is now exponential, those who position themselves in front of the change wave can generate dramatic results in short periods of time. For the prior five thousand years or so before the 1990s, humanity experienced arithmetic change (1 plus 1 plus 1, etc.). Humans were the agent for change then, and we change ever so slowly. Technology is now the agent for change, and the Internet enables geometric change (3 times 4 times 5, etc.). An increasing rate of change means that a very few people can have an overly dramatic impact on their surroundings.

MIDAS MOMENT

More than 100 years ago, the Italian economist Pareto noticed that 20% of Italians owned 80% of that country's wealth. Thus was borne the famous 80/20 rule, also known as a power law. Power laws reign supreme in the Aggregation Age. These laws show that precious few causes generate disproportionate results. The rate of change is so fast today, that now it takes only 5% of the cause to generate 90% of the effect in many important areas, especially productivity and income generation. To the 5% go the spoils.

The following are examples where 5% of the cause generates about 90% of the result:

- About 5% of American business owners are currently generating 90% of the incremental value being created by private firms

- Only 5% of mortgages in the US defaulted to cause 90% of the write-offs in the financial system in 2007

- 5% of authors sell about 90% of all popular press books

- About 5% of venture capital investments generate around 90% of total portfolio returns

- Only 5% of farms in the U.S. produce 90% of the crops

Why does it matter that so few inputs now generate such a large percentage of the outputs? Because in a 90/5 world, power curves, not the more intuitive normal distributions (bell-shaped curves), now explain the new reality: that unexpected events and unusually productive people shape the world. This totally tramples Woody Allen's previously accepted principle that 90% of life is just showing up.

How do these over-achievers do it? In short, they leverage their know-how, also known as intellectual capital. Most people only leverage their know-how on a 1:1 basis, which hopefully enables them to earn a living. For this discussion, let's say they earn $50,000 per year. Super achievers have learned to leverage their intellectual capital by upwards of 50:1, which means they produce 50 times the result of the 1:1 group. In our example, the super achiever earns $2.5 million per year (50 times $50,000). Every business vertical in the world is now being dominated by companies that have learned to leverage their collective know-how beyond their competitors. This explains why the future of business is not China or Europe versus the United States; rather, it's a war won by company versus

MIDAS MOMENT

company. In other words, whoever leverages their intellectual capital the most wins.

A recent book, *The Black Swan* by Nicholas Taleb, sheds light on the importance of the role of unexpected events. The title is a reference to our historical notion that all swans are white. Of course, as is the case with many unexpected and inexplicable events, a flock of black swans were spotted in Australia. Taleb claims that rare events, such as 9/11, or the Bear Sterns meltdown, occur much more often than we expect. Our minds are programmed to deal with what we've seen before, to "expect the expected," so to speak. However, all too often extreme events do indeed take place, and have large and long lasting effects. Black Swan events come in both positive and negative forms. For instance, a break-through of an alternative energy source to oil would be a positive Black Swan. Such an innovation would represent a dramatic leveraging of intellectual capital, with game-changing results.

In a 90/5 world, extreme events will shape the world. But we use averages to guide our thoughts and actions. We create institutions that are built on averages. The current political discussion of possibly redistributing wealth is reflective of our penchant for averages. The same can be said about our educational system, which is often based on a lowest common denominator approach. But all of this is counter to the new reality: in the Aggregation Age extreme events and exceptional people will in large part determine our future.

IN SEARCH OF THE MIDAS TOUCH

I'm often asked, "Can anyone become a Midas Manager?" The answer, I'm sorry to say, is "no." While the strategies herein can be replicated and implemented by any manager in any industry, no book is going to give that manager the Midas touch. Midas Managers are born on life's battlefield, often via some cataclysmic event that occurs early in life. For example, many famous Midas Managers were breadwinners for their families before they turned 13.

Fortunately, you don't need to be a Midas Manager to create substantial wealth. You can copy their architecture and methods, especially when it involves marketing. Architecture is important to this group. This book shows you how to become a "Value Architect," which incorporates the main characteristics that enable Midas Managers to design and deliver value-creating strategies. This is the subject of the next two chapters.

MIDAS MOMENT

2

THE NEWEST RULES

Each business Age spawns its own set of rules. Companies that adopt early and play well by the rules are the big value creators. The few years following an Age change, however, are a dangerous time for the status quo. The world of business is just starting to enter the Aggregation Age. Things are about to get interesting.

Before we consider the Aggregation Age, let's first review the Conceptual Age. There are various ways to describe behavior required for creating wealth in the Conceptual Age. But the most important skills center on the human mind, or, more precisely, on the two hemispheres of the brain. The Information Age worked the left side of our brains, where we do heavy analytical lifting; success in the current Age relies on the right side, the source of our creativity. In his book, *A Whole New Mind: Moving from the Information Age to the Conceptual Age*, author Daniel H. Pink argues that the left brain capabilities that ruled the Information Age, while still necessary, aren't sufficient in the Conceptual Age. The skill sets required now reflect the imperative placed on design, innovation and market knowledge in the 21st century. As children, many of us were told to avoid artistic careers in favor of a more reliable future in business. In the Conceptual Age, our ability to be "artsy" will in large part determine our success in business. In a world where the major resources are available to everyone, it's the ability to do more with less that separates winners from losers.

Companies today compete in a technology-enabled, logistics-powered, globalized economy. Competition is no longer local, it's global, and the rules of value creation have changed. For the purposes of this book I'll use the terms "value" and "wealth" interchangeably, even though there is a timing difference between the two. Value is unrealized wealth. First you build value in a company; then you convert this value to wealth via some liquidity event.

Let's consider some of the New Rules of value creation in the Conceptual Age:

- Every person working in or for a business must create value to remain employed.

- Job security is a function of the number of value-creating skill sets a person possesses.

- A company can expand its returns through arbitrage if its managers understand how to exploit market opportunities.

- Companies should adopt conceptual business models to create wealth. As such, a company should control — not own — its process chain.

- In order to make good investment and financing decisions, and thereby create wealth, managers must raise their Private Finance I.Q.

Although playing by these New Rules will help business owners and managers create wealth, we can't escape the paradoxical nature of the Conceptual Age. This is best illustrated by the first entry in the "rules to consider" section of Wikipedia, the volunteer-written Internet encyclopedia: Ignore all rules.

DAWNING OF THE AGGREGATION AGE

We stand at the cusp of a new Age. The Aggregation Age is launching because the "haves" of the Conceptual Age have figured out how to leverage their knowledge or intellectual capital to a much greater degree than the "have-nots." Much like our capitalistic system, which has created tremendous individual inequality between the wealthy and poor, the same can be said about what has happened inside the world of business. About 5% of businesses have broken from the pack today and are creating the lion's share of the wealth. These lions have caused the Aggregation Age to come about. You need to learn their strategies and tactics now if you're going to keep up.

MIDAS MOMENT

Much of what you're about to read will seem unfamiliar. This is a further indication of how much work you need to do to compete well in this Age. Now let's consider some of the Newest Rules of the Aggregation Age:

Newest Rules of Value Creation in the Aggregation Age

- Managers must design and implement compelling value propositions for all stakeholders of the firm.

- Value propositions should be packaged and positioned in the crowd, customer base, and supply chain.

- Companies should adopt Pull business models to create value. Further, a company should control — not own — its business space.

- Managers should quality control manage their space chains, i.e., keep their fingers on many pulses, but not leave their fingerprints on the space chain or business.

- Managers should become value architects, and thereby leverage their firm's intellectual capital by at least 10:1.

A curious thing has occurred to companies that adopt the Newest Rules: they have eliminated salespeople. For many owners, this fact alone will be enough for them to immediately begin adopting. A later chapter — Death of a Salesman — shows that one company packages its intellectual capital to an extent that, in a three-year period, it more than doubled its annual revenues without benefit of its 12 salespeople.

VALUE PROPOSITIONS

A value proposition answers the question: what's in it for me (WIFM)? To create value in a capitalistic world and Age, owners and managers must create compelling answers to this question for all stakeholders. Notice this doesn't say to create compelling value just for customers: that's so Information Age. These days, managers need to design and deliver WIFM solutions for employees, other shareholders, vendors, advisors, the local community, and yes, customers. Ignore any one of these groups, and that's where the weakness will appear. For example, for years the Big 3 automotive companies have leaned on their supply chains to reduce pricing without giving them

MIDAS MOMENT

equal value. Now large numbers of automotive suppliers are bank-rupt. It's interesting to note that the Japanese and other transplants typically viewed their suppliers as value-added partners; as a result, their supply chains are healthier by comparison.

But don't forget the most important stakeholder — you! This leads to the more descriptive value proposition acronym: WIFUM (what's in it for you and me). Of course you need to create value yourself as you are implementing compelling value propositions for everyone else.

But just creating a value proposition isn't enough; managers also need to package the proposition and insert it into the Company's supply chain, crowd, and customers. In other words, the proposition gets institutionalized in the Company's practices and business model. For instance, a later chapter describes how Back-ers, a T-shirt manufacturer, has created a community of designers and customers. Rather than selling T-shirts to individuals in a retail environment, Backers has no stores with shelves of inventory. In-stead, the company has created a virtual store that attracts some of the best artists in the world to design works of art on their shirts. At the same time the community votes on which designs they prefer, causing a marketing machine that generates predictable (and large) numbers of sales. The key thing here is that Backers has institution-alized its value proposition in such a way that its key managers no longer need to drive the business to create substantial value.

IT'S ABOUT THE PULL

Most of us have pushed our way to success. We push our ideas and value propositions on all who will listen — and on many who won't. We fill our days sending letters and emails and making cold calls. We attempt to push our way into prospective customers' offices. We keep pushing until either a sale occurs or they threaten us with a restraining order. In a noisy world, we wonder why none of our pushing activities seem to work anymore.

The Aggregation Age, like marketing, is about pulling resources and customers to you. You need to create the condition that makes the door swing in to you. This is the secret of marketing in this new Age, literally. The book, *The Secret* by Rhonda Byrne, explains that creating the power of attraction is what separates winners and losers in life. We may correctly call the Aggregation Age the Magnetic Age, where the strongest magnet wins.

In a Pull world, push activities such as traditional sales, public relations, and direct marketing through the mails are being replaced by more effective Pull models. All of the story chapters in this book showcase how Midas Managers pull their stakeholders to achieve their desired outcomes. Chapter 11, in particular, illustrates how one such Manager was able to get his customers to walk through his door — and in a big way.

MIDAS MOMENT

LESS IS MORE

Most owners are control freaks. You know it; I know it. A desire to control their own destinies is what draws most people to business ownership. Somewhat surprisingly, that's a good thing in the Aggregation Age — as long as the owner-managers keep their fingerprints off the business. By definition there's a tendency for control freaks to want to micro-manage, and this is a bad thing for value creation. Midas Managers control their firms by monitoring several metrics, or key performance indicators (KPIs). Thus they keep their fingers on a few pulses, a practice that enables the Manager to work mainly on value-creating activities. Most Midas Managers I know work less than 8 hours each week in a conventional sense. It's purely a matter of working on the right things, and leveraging that time into value-creation.

How does someone practically leverage their intellectual capital to a large degree, say 10:1? Answer: they become value architects. Value architects design, package and implement value-added solutions. They do not actually build the metaphorical house; rather, they hand the design to a general contractor who is responsible for the build-out. The general contractor, who may or may not be an employee, engages the tradespeople, who swing the hammers.

Most business owners begin their careers as tradespeople. They use their skill sets to work as expert mechanics, basically keeping their heads under the hoods. The majority of small business owners never gravitate beyond this hands-on effort. Some tradespeople raise their heads often enough and have enough intellectual curiosity to evolve into general contractors. Most general contractors can manage building 3-to-4 buildings at a time, which is at best a 4:1 leverage. It's extremely difficult to attain financial independence with leverage less than 5:1.

Let's talk about financial independence. I'll define it as having enough money to do whatever you want, whenever you want it. Everyone, of course, has a different idea of how much this is. For instance, recently I met a business owner in New York City who was considering selling his business. He assembled his financial team to help him make this decision. I told him his business was worth $100 million; his CPA told him he would pay roughly $20 million in taxes; his money manager said he could expect interest income of about $5 million per year. The owner considered all of this and then proclaimed: "You expect me to live on $5 million per year?"

But how does one become financially independent? Here's how it works in Midas-ville: Midas Managers choose marketing niches and create compelling architecture with associated value propositions; they attract the best general contractors; they make sure the firm's processes are completely efficient, i.e., the company owns its intellectual capital but controls its space; and then they choose strategies that provide the maximum leverage to its intellectual capital. There — it's that easy.

The next chapter discusses value architecture and value propositions.

MIDAS MOMENT

INVESTMENT BANKER MAN

Not a great value proposition for IBMan

3

VALUE ARCHITECTURE 101

Ultimately, our fierce, Darwinian form of capitalism breaks down to one guiding question for the players: what's in it for me (WIFM)? Companies that tune into this station and answer the question successfully for all of their stakeholders can create substantial value. Why? Because the answer to this question is also the company's value proposition.

Many Marketing textbooks propose that companies should offer a compelling value proposition only to customers. This is just part of the story (granted, an important one). Unless a company considers the value it brings to all stakeholders, it won't have the best employees, vendors, outside resources, etc. In other words, it won't have all of the people who make a business special. Designing and delivering compelling value propositions to all stakeholders, while still earning a fair profit, is an owner's Number 1 job (remember WIFUM). This can't be outsourced. In order to accomplish this Herculean task, an owner needs to become a value architect.

How do you know if you're a value architect? You are such a person if you meet the following conditions: you could be away from your business for months at a time without hurting the company; you rarely have your fingerprints on anything in the business; you could properly be called an Active Chairperson of your company; and you're almost totally strategic toward your company. And yes, you're either financially independent or on the path to it.

Midas Managers are value architects. They create the structure that enables substantial value creation in a business. Specifically, they do the following: 1) design and package a compelling value proposition for all stakeholders (including themselves, of course); 2) rationalize their company's space chain (they own their intellectual capital, but control as much of their space or sphere of influence as is economically appropriate); 3) choose strategies that leverage their intellectual capital; 4) keep their fingers on the pulse of the business. The actual management and implementation of the architecture is delegated to general contractors — who may or may not be employees of the firm. General contractors attract and oversee the appropriate resources to build the architecture.

Continuing with this building analogy, most small business owners are tradespeople (e.g., carpenters). They learn a set of skills, and use the expert model to generate and conduct business. They are purely tactical - meaning that the owner can make a living, but not create wealth, for that requires strategic thinking and action. By definition, tactical means low leverage. Many years ago my dad, an owner of a mid-sized construction company, told me that most people learn some skills on their first job, but don't progress much beyond that point during their career. I didn't think this was possible. But lifetime tradespeople prove his point.

Many tradespeople owners convert into general contractors (GC's). This conversion is probably caused due to the tradesperson getting tired of working incredibly long hours, with little more to show for it than a decent salary. At some point, these people realize that to get ahead they need to move upstream from the purely expert model. GC's leverage their intellectual capital enough to create a lifestyle, but usually don't create substantial value in the business.

GC's put their fingerprints on most parts of their business, which creates a constraint on growth and value creation.

How does one become a value architect? Converting to a value architect from a GC is more revolutionary than evolutionary. This is because value architecture demands a total change in behavior; it's about thinking, planning, and overseeing. These are quite different skills from those needed by a general contractor, which are far more activity-based and control-oriented. Many GC's will need mentoring from a value architect to become a value architect themselves.

Let's review each value architecture step in more detail.

Step #1: Design and Package Compelling Value Propositions

It takes some work determining an answer to the WIFM question for each stakeholder. Of course, the best place to start is to ask each player what they want out of the relationship. It's amazing how often this conversation is assumed, but not directly undertaken.

The WIFM question cannot be fully answered until it is understood what makes people tick. This, of course, requires some fairly

MIDAS MOMENT

serious psychological assessment. Carl Jung said that the meeting of two personalities is like the contact of two chemical substances: if there is any reaction, both are transformed. Midas Managers seem somewhat old-fashioned in this personal chemistry area, relying on track records and incentives, as opposed to using tests and outside experts.

In the past twenty years we've moved far from the land of "a good kick in the butt is all they need" management to more of a touchy-feely style. It can be a lot of work to quickly determine and then fulfill the needs of various personality types. This probably explains why Midas Managers only perform this task with the people in their direct line of sight. Personality matching and feeding is delegated — but overseen — to the general contractors for the remainder of the stakeholders.

Entering the marketplace with an enticing value proposition is still first among equals. The next chapter describes how to design a black hole niche - the most powerful of Pull marketing strategies.

Value propositions must also be packaged. This means they must be institutionalized in the architecture, so that the WIFM question is routinely answered during the course of business. Here is an example of value proposition packaging: customers get exactly what they ordered, when they ordered it, at an agreed-upon quality level; general contractors for the firm are incentivized to behave in a way that adds to the value of the firm and to themselves; tradespeople understand what is expected of them and what they will receive for giving it; and all other resources feel they are being fairly treated by the firm as well as providing value to it. This kind of value proposition packaging needs to be standard operating procedure, forming, in effect, the culture of the company.

Step #2: Rationalize your Space Chain

A goal of the Conceptual Age is to "rationalize your process chain." This means you should own unique capabilities (intellectual capital), and outsource everything else. You create wealth in a business when you learn to leverage your intellectual capital to a greater degree than your competition. Non-value-adding steps should be outsourced, but controlled. As a general rule, steps that don't create value should be undertaken within a company (not outsourced) only when: a) no outside vendor is available; b) the cost of outsourcing is prohibitive; or c) confidentiality forbids it.

In the Aggregation Age, all major competitors have rationalized their process chains. This is no longer a goal for them; it's a reality. These companies are now rationalizing their space chains. A space chain represents the steps in the supply chain that are within the company's sphere of influence. More specifically, these are the steps in which it makes economic sense for a company to aggregate. In days of yore, we might call this activity either horizontal or vertical integration. But integration means ownership. Aggregation means control. Controlling your space allows you to exert tremendous influence over it without the risk or cost of owning the

MIDAS MOMENT

resource that does the job. The final four chapters of this book show how to control a space without owning it.

Step #3: Select Leveraging Strategies

Midas Managers say that once you decide where you are in a business, and determine where you want to go, the appropriate strategies to get there always reveal themselves. So the "how" to meet a goal is not a constraint. But what should non-Midas Managers do? They either need to find a mentor to help them decide which strategies are appropriate, or copy the strategies of Midas Managers. But beware: never copy a strategy unless that strategy is intuitive to you. We all get lost in the conceptual woods from time-to-time, and strategies provide the map to get through the woods. If the strategy is intuitive, you'll naturally figure out the path. If you see yourself in one or more of the stories in this book, that's a strong clue that you've found your intuitive strategy.

Step #4: Only Fingers on the Pulse

Tradespeople and general contractors put their fingerprints all over a business. Nothing can happen in their businesses unless they touch it. Value architects, on the other hand, rarely put their fingerprints on their businesses. Rather, they have their fingers on the pulses of the business. They use metrics to monitor performance of the critical success factors (CSFs) that drive the value of the firm. CSFs are the big things that have to go right to make a business successful. These are things like market acceptance, customer counts, new product development, etc. CSFs are higher level activities than Key Performance Indicators (KPIs), such as sales per employee hours worked, gross profit margins by product line, etc. KPIs are the metrics used to measure the financial and non-financial actions in the firm that drive and support the critical success factors.

The difference between CSFs and KPIs is important because it ties into the strategic methodology of assessing the company's ability to create value. Breaking metrics into two levels allows strategy to be evaluated at the CSF level, and tactics to be implemented and measured at the KPI level. It forces the business owner to begin thinking strategically about CSFs, and tactically to measure the results of tactical implementation through KPIs.

Architects understand that they lose leverage when they grab hold of the details. Of course, even architects need to fingerprint the business from time to time. But these periods are short-lived, and usually the architect institutionalizes a response so that handling the tactical doesn't become routine.

Showing you what's necessary to convert from a general contractor to a value architect is one of the primary goals of this book. Financial independence awaits those who make this transition. You can do this.

The next chapter describes how to pull the necessary customers and resources to you.

MIDAS MOMENT

4

BLACK HOLE NICHES

My name is Rob, and I'm a niche-aholic. There — I admit it. You can say "Hi, Rob" to me later. Right now, the most important thing is for you to also become a niche-aholic. This chapter starts your journey.

A wise business owner once told me that successful service providers create a condition where the door to their office swings in, not the other way around. In other words, the clients come to them. A Pull business model creates this condition. All of the stories in this book demonstrate how Midas Managers pull rather than push.

There's still no better way to pull customers than to become a niche-aholic firm. I'm talking about creating "black hole niches," super-powerful forces that have customers and stakeholders wishing you'll never go out of business because it would hurt them. Here's the traditional description of an astronomical black hole: a star system expands too fast and collapses into itself with such gravitational attraction that not even light can escape. Now the marketing black hole niche: a company's value propositions and services are so compelling, stakeholders prefer to be caught in the vortex of attraction rather than try to escape. This is Midas Marketing at its best!

How does one create a black hole niche? Niche-aholics set their dials to WIFM and play the music loudly — for all to hear. They determine, for each group of stakeholders, what proposition is so strong that the stakeholder will gladly give up their gravitational sovereignty. Chapter 9 shows how one company uses a "give-it-away" strategy that entices prospective customers to want to become paying customers. In fact, customers willingly pay for the privilege of being able to buy from this company.

Historically, companies have pushed their offerings rather than pulled. During the Industrial Age, firms pushed their products and services onto an unempowered customer base. Sellers took advantage of the limited choices offered in the market. Things began to change in the Information Age, as technology enabled buyers to select from a multitude of sellers. Buyers took control during the Conceptual Age; they began to pull solutions to them rather than accept what was pushed at them. Chris Anderson, in his wonderful book, *The Long Tail*, describes the niche strategy of businesses such as Amazon or Netflix that sell a large number of unique items in relatively small quantities. The people who buy the hard-to-find or "non-hit" items is the customer demographic called the Long Tail. And they number in the billions. The tipping point has now been reached - the Aggregation Age is strictly a Pull age. And most companies aren't ready to make this transition.

John Hagel, a specialist on pull platforms, says the pull is starting at the edge of an enterprise, rather than deep inside it, because it is here that the greatest uncertainty lies. It's also here that push models, with their assumption of centralized control, are less viable (unless a company has enormous market power like Wal-Mart). Pull platforms are also beginning to take hold in such emerging economies as China and India because these platforms are particularly powerful in supporting bootstrapping activity. Hagel claims pull platforms are emerging at the demographic edge; younger generations more comfortable with the technologies and tools emerging on electronic networks are pioneering both the creation and use of pull platforms to create businesses that grow extremely fast with relatively modest investment.

The Internet provides the backbone for communities to coalesce around pull ideas. Look no farther than the development of Wikipedia, the open-source encyclopedia, to see how thousands of users can work together for a common good. Knowledge creation now transcends company boundaries. In fact, innovation and creativity are being distributed across firms with the idea that if two heads are better than one, then a million heads should be the goal. But achieving this requires platforms that harness common interests.

Like *Midas Managers*, this is a story book. But this book is all about the Pull. Story chapters are organized into three groups: 1) Pull the crowd; 2) Pull the customer; 3) Aggregate your space.

MIDAS MOMENT

PULL THE CROWD

The Aggregation Age demonstrates the evolution of open sourcing. There's no better example of this collaborative notion than crowdsourcing. With crowdsourcing, you take a task traditionally performed by an employee or contractor, and outsource it to an undefined, generally large group of people, in the form of an open call. The public may be invited to develop a new technology, carry out a design task, refine an algorithm or help capture, systematize or analyze large amounts of data. Often the group is compensated in some way. For example, Netflix announced that they were offering a $1,000,000 prize for anybody who could improve their existing DVD rating system by at least 10%. Typically, crowdsourcing relies on volunteers working in their spare time, or from small businesses which were unknown to the initiating organization.

The difference between crowdsourcing and ordinary outsourcing is that a task or problem is outsourced to the public, rather than to another body. In crowdsourcing, the activity is initiated by a client, and the work may be undertaken on an individual, as well as a group, basis. Think of it this way: traditional outsourcing enables control over a process chain; whereas, crowdsourcing enables control over a space.

It turns out that the world has good ideas, open capacity, and a desire to participate. Crowdsourcing is evolving from groups doing the work, to groups providing the designs, doing the work, and providing the customer base. This is leading to the concept of viral equity — where the crowd takes ownership of the products and services of the sponsoring company. Perhaps no better example of this holistic plug-in is YourBrew Beer, the company profiled in Chapter 7. YourBrew, a specialty beer if there ever was one, was designed and literally consumed by its community.

PULL THE CUSTOMER

Even in the Aggregation Age, most commerce will not be driven by the crowd. Attracting individual customers is still in vogue. Imagine that. Fortunately, technology empowers companies to pull customers via a compelling value proposition like never before.

So how do you get a customer to walk through your door? Let's first talk about what doesn't work. Main Street companies typically don't have the resources for old-fashioned "push" marketing campaigns, such as PR (public relations) and advertising. These ways of attracting customers are too expensive and usually aren't cost-effective. Before I knew better, I used PR to push *Midas Managers* soon after it came out. As far as I can tell, it cost me roughly $1,000 in PR expense for each copy sold. That experience taught me that PR and other push-based marketing initiatives are no longer effective.

A paradox of "Pull" marketing is that an initial "push" is required. In order to get your value proposition out there, you need to make sure the right people know about it. This can be done by identifying and incentivizing "market makers." Market makers are people or institutions who already have access to the starving crowd. So Makers provide the

MIDAS MOMENT

push into the prospective affinity group. Makers are not employees, which makes them even more valuable for our purposes.

Let's consider a market making example. Let's say a lawyer faces the issue of how to make a market for her legal services. Lawyers have historically had a difficult time marketing their services due to ethical and other experiential difficulties. But this lawyer — let's call her Jane — does something interesting and unexpected. She goes to several executive directors of trade associations and cuts a deal with them. Her firm will provide a bundle of estate planning services for a fairly low fixed fee. Jane will provide a package of services that all pro-crastinating business owners need, for about half the price their own lawyers would charge. Plus Jane will run free educational seminars for the owners and their spouses so they can get their minds around the issues. The executive directors willingly act as market makers because they are helping their members. With this arrangement, Jane now has more than 5,000 captive prospective clients, enough for her to create a machine to package her deliverables. Jane does all of this because she understands the nature of providing upfront deliverables: her firm will also provide the back-end services for many of the clients, and that's where the real money can be made.

There are numerous other ways to attract customers. For in-stance, Chapter 13 shows how one owner "sets the hook" for pro-spective customers by so involving them in the design of high-end dresses that customers basically take ownership of the designs. The offer to participate is so irresistible that customers just have to bite. This strategy is inherent in black hole niches. It involves three sim-ple steps: 1) create an irresistible offer; 2) attract a hungry crowd; 3) set up the buffet. Successful restaurants have been doing this for years, but the strategy is available to every type of business.

AGGREGATE YOUR SPACE

Successful companies control — not own — their space. It's just too expensive, and not very efficient, to acquire and own everything. *Midas Managers* states that companies need to control - not own — their process chains. A process chain represents all of the process steps a company needs to perform in order to deliver its product or service. By "rationalizing" your process chain, you own your intellectual capital and outsource the non-value-added steps. In the Aggregation Age, all value-creating competitors have already rationalized their process chains. Now companies need to control as much of their supply chain as is appropriate. Aggregators will create substantial value in this Age; aggregatees will often just work for a living. Hence, the name of this new Age.

Aggregators come in two primary forms: 1) market intermediaries, and 2) modular consolidators. Market intermediaries bring together a broad spectrum of customer needs and provide the interface and tools for customers to buy what they need. Customers have autonomy to select what they need. Think Amazon and eBay. Amazon, in particular, has evolved past pure intermediation, and

MIDAS MOMENT

now offers fuller marketplace options to its customers, including allowing specialized retailers to piggyback on its exchange. Market intermediation benefits from the Long Tail phenomenon mentioned above. There is a large audience for unusual items.

Modular consolidators are true to their names: they create modules of products or services and insert them into the supply chain. Historically we have called such firms system integrators. Think about Boeing. Boeing designed the Dreamliner jet, and then outsourced the engineering to Russia, the fuselage design and modules to Japan, the interior cabinetry modules to Brazil, etc. All of the various modules are shipped to Seattle, where Boeing integrates them into a new airplane. In the Aggregation Age, successful companies take system integration to the next level: they become space integrators.

During the Conceptual Age, we started moving from a push-based era of command-and-control management; now, we're heading into an era where more and more work is being conducted using a decentralized, pull-based model that is more scalable, efficient, and leads to increasingly innovative outcomes. In the Aggregation Age, moving day is over.

In this exponentially changing Age, the future is now. Midas Managers and their marketing strategies form the edge. William Smith has it right, however, when he says: "the future is already here, it is just unevenly distributed."

The next chapter summarizes the stories that describe how to pull the crowd.

INVESTMENT BANKER MAN

A tall tale mocking the long tail

5

PULL THE CROWD

t's ironic that, in the Aggregation Age, the more people are physically disconnected from each other, the more they seek connection through communities. Web-based communities, especially, thrive because the members share some affinity or passion. It may be the only place members can go to be with others like themselves. Paradoxically, this open sharing often happens behind a veil of personal anonymity. In any event, the crowd for your value proposition is waiting and wanting to be pulled.

The following four chapters describe how various individuals created communities. They not only attracted a crowd — they also put them to work! In something of an Aggregation Age scam, members of a well-structured community feel the need to contribute to the point of doing most of the lifting. The organizer needs merely to light up the crowd.

Here's a brief synopsis of the next four chapters.

Chapter 6: Giving the Shirts Off Our Backs

In something of a Midas first, this chapter compares and contrasts the behavior and models of two players in the same industry — t-shirt retailing. The first player takes a traditional path of owning everything to get to his goal, including all the designs, the means of production, and the physical retail locations. The second company owns little, except its website. Designs for this second company are created by the community, which also decides winners from losers. The community then buys the winners, creating an instant market for their choices. Guess which company prospers and which one doesn't?

Chapter 7: This Beer's For Us

Since it deals with beer drinking, this story may be my favorite in the book. I grew-up in the road construction industry, where all things were measured by beer consumption. A "kegger" job meant we would be moving a mountain, whereas a six-pack job meant something quick. So a story about a down-on-his-luck guy who launches a beer company is right up my alley (so to speak). Of course he doesn't create a traditional brew; he creates a community beer company, where the community designs the beer, the bottle, label and language used to describe it. Talk about generating a community buzz.

Chapter 8: There's Gold in Them Thar Hills

What would you do if you were CEO of a mining company that can no longer find gold? Before you answer, consider that your company owns more than 50,000 acres that for decades has yielded literally tons of gold. But now you can't find enough gold to keep the doors open. The answer: offer 100% of your proprietary geologic mining data to the public — in the hopes that non-miners can tell you where your gold is. Sounds crazy, right? Crazy like a gold-plated fox. Sorry. This story is solid crowdsourcing gold.

Chapter 9: Just Give It Away

If you believe it's better to give than receive, you'll like this story. Sometimes you just need to give your product or service away until enough members of your community are addicted. This is the time-honored push-first, then-pull game. The real beauty of this game is that, once addicted to your value proposition, the community will pay for the privilege of buying your stuff. Does it get any better than this?

The concept of crowdsourcing is strewn and exemplified throughout these four chapters. What an idea, that the crowd knows more than experts in a field; that the crowd can create and consume your products. I'm all over this. This notion is extremely important to me, as Chapter 19 illustrates. Do yourself a big favor: go attract and empower a crowd in your business.

MIDAS MOMENT

INVESTMENT BANKER MAN

What could the crowd possibly know?

6

GIVING THE SHIRTS OFF OUR BACKS

Jack Smithson was born into the retail business. His parents ran a men's clothing store inherited from Jack's grandfather, a highly skilled Saville Row tailor. Jack's father gloried in telling stories of his struggle to modernize the business by introducing ready to wear suits into the shop. Jack, however, despised the long hours and unrewarded efforts of his parents. He felt his talent and the future was in design.

Jack considers himself an individual with great style and a leader of the great counterculture movement. Black on black started as a convenient wardrobe choice, but grew into a chains-&-leather, gothic mode of expression, while his parents became more scandalized and critical. Nothing like parental disapproval to encourage a rebel. In high school, Jack quickly learned that girls were attracted to his bad boy loner image. When they learned that he could design and actually produce his costumes, he became something of a counterculture pop star. Jack decided to profit from his notoriety and started a business — Kill Or Be Killed (KOBK) Kouture. After all, biker buddies and vampire chicks need outfitting, too.

Jack opened a store supplying paraphernalia, clothing and all manner of items that polite society might find offensive. Over time, he expanded to several retail stores, opened a manufacturing facility to forge belt buckles and other metal accessories, and started a joint venture with an Indian firm to supply his KOBK-designed shirts. After five years, he owned six storefronts, and KOBK tee-shirts were the best selling "street" brand in the country.

Jack had a good eye for design and had kept the company in front of the design curve since it was founded. Unfortunately, Jack's loner genius image was also his management style. He tried other designers along the way, both employees and outsiders, but no one else had his feel for the product lines. One of the young designers he had interned attempted to convince Jack that a new world was coming to product design — a collaborative world. Jack, though, would have none of it. No one was going to interfere with his KOBK brand.

CUT FROM A DIFFERENT CLOTH

The young designer — Tom Peterson — would not be denied. He had a splinter in his mind, and the only way to remove it was to act. He called one of his buddies, Bingo Baker, to check his temperature about opening a clothing company. Bingo was an energy guy and naturally lucky, having earned his nickname after a well-timed 'B-6' was called.

As luck would have it, there was a tee-shirt design competition taking place on the Net to design the official tee for an event to take place in Rome. Tom and Bingo won, beating out more than 500 other web product designers. Thus was born a new company — Backers.

The Backers boys started talking online about how awesome it was to participate in the competition. Soon, they were part of an on-line community of thousands of art and design people who shared and critiqued each others' work. It was a very creative environment all around for hobbyists and professionals alike to unleash their creativity in their free time. Backers was created to "give back" to the community by producing goods drawn from the work created by these artists. Tom and Bingo started it as a hobby, as a way to play in this online community. So they borrowed money from family and launched a site.

Backers hosted its first tee-shirt design competition a few months after their big design win. They started a thread on their site asking people to make tee-shirt designs, after which they would print the winning designs, put them up for sale, and use the profits to hold another competition and print more winning designs.

Backers spent about $1,000 printing two dozen examples of five different designs chosen from those submitted on the Backers thread. For the first few rounds, the winning designers received a few free copies of their winning tee and that was it. After six months, winning designers also received $100 cash.

For the first year, the tee-shirt printer shipped orders for Backers. By the second year, Backers stocked all the tees in Tom's apartment. Tom and Bingo would meet once a week to package that week's orders, and then ship them out the following day. For those

MIDAS MOMENT

first two years, every dime they earned from selling tees went right back into printing more of them.

Backers ran design competitions through an online social network. Members of the network submitted their ideas for tee-shirts — hundreds each week — and then voted on which ones they liked best. Hundreds of thousands of people were using the site as a kind of community center, where they blogged, chatted about designs, socialized with their fellow enthusiasts — and bought a ton of shirts at $15 each. Revenue was growing 500 percent a year, despite the fact that the company had never advertised, employed no professional designers, used no modeling agency or fashion photographers, had no sales force, and enjoyed no retail distribution. As a result, costs were low, margins were above 30 percent, and — because community members told them precisely which shirts to make — every product eventually sold out.

GETTING KILLED

Something unexpected was happening across town at Kill Or Be Killed: it was getting killed. Jack was losing control over his empire. Costs were up at the factory, and cheap knock-offs were flooding the market. It seems KOBK had drawn the attention of the new Barbary pirates, the Far Eastern counterfeiters.

At the same time, the grunge look was on its way out. The Woodstock generation was aging out from their 1960s ways, while young people were after a different look - something fresher, less assassin-like. But Jack had only one design path, and that road was now blocked. Plus, he had run off all of his younger designers. It wasn't clear to Jack what he should do on that front. One thing was clear: the factory had to go, so he shut that down. Plus he shuttered a couple of his stores. Jack felt very lonely.

Less than a mile away, Backers was growing by leaps and bounds. This was true in the number of employees, warehouse space, tees being sold, designs being chosen per week, prizes being awarded to designers, etc. Tom and Bingo were feeling the exhilaration of playing the game at fast-forward speed. Finally, the game got a little too fast, so Backers partnered with a logistics firm that could handle the fulfillment side of the business. This freed up Tom, especially, to focus on the creative side of the business. Two years into this adventure, the prize for a winning design was up to $2,000 in cash and prizes.

From the beginning, Tom and Bingo were guided by a simple credo: they did what felt right and what they thought would be cool to do. So this led them to create their own private label tee-shirt, set up crazy retail stores (they call them community centers), tried to do more for their international customers by getting shipping times and costs down, furthered Backers Kids and a bunch of other random things.

MIDAS MOMENT

Within a mere three-year period, Kill or Be Killed lost nearly half its sales, and was hemorrhaging money. Backers, on the other hand, had grown its sales beyond KOBK's. Thousands of artists hung out and contributed to Backers' community. Hundreds of thousands of people in the community visited the site and bought tees each month — about $30 million dollars worth in a year, with more than $10 million in profits. It churned out dozens of new items a month — with no advertising, no professional designers, no sales force and no retail distribution. And it has never produced a flop.

It turns out that a few thousand minds are better than one.

BLUEPRINT

This chapter is a tale of two marketing approaches, one relying on a traditional model of owning everything, the other leveraging the community. You may recognize that in real life Backers is Threadless — a Chicago company that revolutionized the tee-shirt business.

Threadless is at the vanguard of a new innovation model that is quietly reshaping a host of industries. Whether it's called user innovation, crowdsourcing, or open source, it means drastically rethinking your relationship with your customers. "Threadless completely blurs that line of who is a producer and who is a consumer," says Karim Lakhani, a professor at Harvard Business School. "The customers end up playing a critical role across all its operations: idea generation, marketing, sales forecasting. All that has been distributed."

This idea goes against a basic principle that has been taught in business schools since the invention of mass production: Employees make stuff, and customers buy it. But this notion seems anachronistic in a marketplace of ever-narrowing niches and nearly unlimited consumer choices. Meanwhile, a generation of so-called Web 2.0 companies has succeeded by encouraging customers to contribute to, and in some cases create, the product being sold. Not only do we have instantaneous access to countless television programs through video websites, but anyone with a YouTube account and a digital camera can create a show of his or her own. Professionally edited, dead-tree newspapers are besieged by digital news sites that are produced and edited by their readers. The 240-year-old Encyclopedia Britannica finds itself eclipsed — at least in terms of readership — by Wikipedia.com, which pays its writers nothing and doesn't require that they possess any expertise at all.

Follow these steps to build a user community of designers and buyers:

It's about the community

The sponsors need to create a compelling value proposition for the community. Most of the members work for free, so they must feel that they're getting value for their time. Sponsors need to check their egos at the door, something that limits many from playing this role.

The next chapter talks more about crowdsourcing as a concept.

Provide the tools

Threadless attracts a lot of talent to its contests. The contest format encourages artists to tell their less artistic friends about the site. Designers labor mightily on their submissions; they spend weeks tinkering with their works and soliciting advice from other members. Then they post links to their submissions on their websites, blogs, and MySpace pages, asking their friends to click, vote, and, the artists hope, buy. Threadless helps with this, sending the artists digital submission kits that include HTML code and graphics to help them create professional-looking advertisements for their designs.

Keep it fresh

In real life, Tom Peterson is named Jake Nickell. He is a founder and still the driving force behind Threadless. Nickell says a certain amount of tension is inevitable in community-based businesses. "Even before now, we've been losing our core people and gaining new core people," he says. "It's kind of like a band in its infancy: As soon as a lot of people start listening to the band, the core fans go away." Nickell points out that the look of Threadless' tee-shirts — what other clothing companies might call the brand — has changed drastically, as his audience has evolved from a small collection of geeky Web designers to include tens of thousands of teenagers from middle America. Webmaster jokes have been re-placed by cultural references; wordplay has given way to painterly richness. The Threadless brand is not the shirts but the community experience. As Nickell puts it, "Our brand is a fun boys' and girls' club."

Expand the playground.

Now, Nickell is set to let his club loose on other businesses. In addition to expanding to children's clothing and retail, Threadless will begin selling prints and posters online. And later this year, the company will add a range of products, including handbags, wallets, and dinnerware, under the brand Naked & Angry. Each item will be adorned with patterns submitted by users, with a new product launched each month.

MIDAS MOMENT

Most of us beyond the age of 40 years were taught to play our cards close to our vest, not only to prevent our competition from trumping us, but also to insure that our employees couldn't see the full picture. Managing in an open source age, however, rewards quite the opposite behavior. I speak more than 50 times each year. In each talk, as with just about everything else, I show all of my cards to the audience; mainly for free or at little cost to the attendees. I know what you're thinking at this point: this guy is not playing with a full deck — so how many cards could he have? I fully accept that I'm not playing with a full deck — that is why I show the cards that I do have. My hope is that attendees will engage me by showing their cards (they're not playing with full decks either), so together we can make a pretty good hand. Or, using the vernacular of this chapter, give the shirts off our backs.

7

THIS BEER'S FOR US

Tom Lilly had just finished his third career move in the past six years. After stints as a web designer and engineer on a social networking site, Tom had recently failed in his first attempt at business ownership. His "Roses by the Dozen" site had not caught on. After 18 months of pushing, Tom had finally shuttered the URL. He was low on funds, and thinking about re-entering the cubicle'd workforce. Now it was time to figure out what had gone wrong, and regroup to determine his next move.

NOT COMING UP ROSES

It was clear to Tom that eCommerce would replace traditional retailing. Proof was all around. Amazon, eBay, and Google had shown the way. Millions of smaller niche eTail sites had popped up. This was a modern-day virtual gold rush.

Tom understood niches on the Net. He had some personal work experience, plus he had more than a dozen friends who were running niche sites on the side. It seemed to him that everyone under 30 years old was Net moonlighting. The key to eNiche-building, Tom knew, doesn't lie in the technical aspects of the site; rather, success depends on the choice of niche and how to build a following. Tom had been looking for an eNiche for about a year when Providence intervened. A girl Tom was dating was a part-time florist. She made a strong case that flowers could be eNiched, because guys were always forgetting to order them for special occasions and they were too busy or too lazy to then stop by a florist. Ordering off the Net was a perfect solution.

Tom did some homework on who was offering flowers on the Net. There were several major players already. Companies like "1-800-Flowers" were offering both phone and Net solutions. They were apparently a truly virtual source, in that they took orders, and then sent the orders to real florists for delivery. It seemed to Tom that these aggregators were pushing a large number of alternative flower arrangements, betting that the customers either wouldn't care to build their own bouquets or were just too busy to create them. Tom ordered flowers from several different companies. The Net interfaces were fairly intuitive and easy to use. And he received what he ordered in just a couple of days. He thought it was a pretty good value for $30-50 per order.

But Tom figured the Net wholesalers had an Achilles heel: they offered too many options - too many different flowers arranged in too many ways. It was information overload. Most guys, he figured, wanted just a couple of options. He figured his niche would be roses. Thus was born "Rosesbythedozen.com."

Creating the site was expensive, but manageable. Tom had several friends who could help, plus it wasn't particularly difficult to get florists around the country to accept his orders. Getting the word out that his site existed was the trickier, and more costly, task. Tom bought key words from Google and Yahoo, plus advertised in a number of airline magazines and other publications he thought men were likely to read.

Between building the site and spending on advertising, Tom

was tapped out. On top of that, the orders were just dribbling in. After 3-to-4 months in eTailing, Tom was seeing the hidden barrier to entering this activity. Anyone with a few bucks could get into business, but making money was a different deal. Unless the eTailer could constantly light up the customer base, orders were few and far between. Plus, it was turning out that merely offering roses to men had been a mistake. A large percentage of women don't care for roses. With little money and no consumer following, rosesbythedozen.com had no future.

A BEER-TER WAY?

Tom was a true believer in web-based commerce, even though traditional eTailing had been a bust for him. He felt that his approach had been wrong. He hadn't studied market behavior enough, which had led him to some major blunders. He didn't know flowers, and somewhere along the way he had even lost his florist girlfriend. Plus, he was now out of money. He needed to leverage his know-how. And what Tom knew was beer.

MIDAS MOMENT

He didn't know beer in any business sense. He just knew that he loved to drink the stuff. Over the years, it was both a hobby and a passion to see how many different worldwide brands he could imbibe. By his count, the number now totaled more than 200. His father had always told Tom to follow his passion and the money would come. It was time to test that theory.

To some, no money and an insatiable thirst for beer might not be the best platform for a business launch. But Tom had learned something from the thorny rose fiasco. He needed to reverse the build-out order: instead of the attitude of "if you build it, they will come," Tom would let the community build his site and brand. For Tom knew the beer drinkers' credo: they loved to talk about beer almost as much as they liked to drink it. Thus was born YourBrew Beer.

IF WE BUILD IT, WE WILL COME

Tom would build a community of beer drinkers. They would design the beer and packaging, and become the group that would drink it. As Tom would say, "YourBrew is the only beer company built by the people for the people."

The beer industry is dominated by a few brewing companies that control over 90% of the market. So going toe-to-toe with the giants was not going to work. That would result in the flower fiasco all over again. Taking a brutally frank approach to the industry, Tom voiced his understanding that he would need to do things differently: "No fancy crap about 'imported hops,' 'first crop barley' or 'mountain water.' It's beer. You get drunk, fall over, start a fight and mosey on out of town." Tom clearly understood the behavior of beer drinkers.

Tom pitched his idea to 150 friends and associates. All were within the 18-35-year-old age group, noted for their comfort with the Internet and fondness for beer. With help from his friends, Tom launched a basic website. Within weeks, they had more than 10,000 people registered and invited them to put down their mugs long enough to create a beer. Since they could vote on alcohol content, taste and bottle design, the participants received "viral equity," taking in dividends based on the beer's sales. Thus the demand was created before the beer, and those who bought a case would get a share of the company.

In just a couple of years following launch, YourBrew experienced the following results:

● YourBrew beer was sold over the Internet to more than 50,000 shareholding customers.

● YourBrew Company sold beer branded with corporate logos for company functions, promotions and gifts; this succeeded to the point of accounting for 50% of sales.

MIDAS MOMENT

● The company boasted "members" in 50 countries. Of course, the beer manufacturing was outsourced.

● Customers could enjoy the company's signature YourBrew brand as is, or design their own labels, created online with a choice of colors and graphics. Ensuring customer satisfaction, YourBrew Company would refund the cost of any unused beer in return for feedback on the product. While the product, as Tom admits, is still beer, its innovative branding and marketing strategies are enough to leave its competitors absolutely parched.

BLUEPRINT

In real life, YourBrew Beer is Brewtopia, a virtual beer company head-quartered in Australia. As its website states, "Brewtopia is a publicly listed company (NSX) whose main business is the promotion of products in a fun, new, conceptual way. Our focus is on the customers' experience in the consumption of goods and services. Our system is built on leveraging the increasing involvement of the consumer to the advantage of the con-sumer."

I'm not sure if Brewtopia's founders experienced a flowery learning curve, but I suspect they floundered in a similar way before launching their virtual beer. In the book, *Testify!*, Liam Mulhall, one of the Brewtopia founders, gives the following steps to create a beer such as Blowfly (the actual brand).

Sell the experience

Offer "The Ride" to the people first — empower them. Let them behind the curtain to make decisions on the development of the product from informa-tion that you give them.

Keep it simple

The premise "Own the beer you drink" was available to everyone. Give the customer an emotional attachment, through their decision-making, and a physical ownership — give them some form of ownership. This creates a cause, plus provides viral and possibly other equity to participants.

Incentives spread the word

Brewtopia used "Beer owned by the people" to spread among a network of friends. Every one that partook received additional share allocations, plus they were invited to the launch of their beer. This activity built the buzz (pun intended) for the brand.

Adjust policy, content or messages based on feedback

Most companies don't realize that customers rarely think about their company the same way they do. Creating a community can only occur when the participants not only take ownership for success, but are empowered to do so.

It should be no surprise that Brewtopia is leveraging its model to expand into custom branded waters, wines, and even champagnes. That's one of the beautiful things about pull marketing models: they are absolutely scalable. And in Brewtopia's case, this means the profits are flowing.

INVESTMENT BANKER MAN

Public relations - pushing to the end

8

THERE'S GOLD IN THEM THAR HILLS

en Harold was a modern day 49er. His entire life had been spent in search of gold, an endeavor he loved, and now he found himself the CEO of Precious Metals Inc. (PMI). But times were not good at the company. Once, PMI had been a major supplier of gold and other precious metals, but in recent years, the company had fallen on hard times. Rocked by strikes, large debts, and high production costs, the company had actually halted mining operations. The market for gold was down as well. Prices were falling at the time, and most observers assumed the company's 50-year-old mine in Canada was dying. Unless some new deposits were discovered soon, PMI would likely follow Sutter's Mill into lore.

Ben was determined to save the company, but as he weighed his options, it seemed that everything was against the company. Its remote Canadian land holdings insured a company culture of self-reliance. The management team was ancient, and Ben suspected they would all run out with a pan in their hands in search of a stream if given half a chance. The company owned or leased more than 50,000 acres, which in the prior 20 years had yielded more gold per acre than any other mine in the world. But as Ben reviewed internal geologist reports, it was clear they couldn't reliably estimate the value and location of the gold on the property. It was time for bold action.

Ben did something unexpected: he left the field of battle. He went east and sought help to solve his dilemma. Ben couldn't even explain why he went to the two-day seminar, but desperate times require desperate actions. Of all things, he found what he was looking for in something called "crowdsourcing." Ben learned that crowdsourcing is the promise of the Internet; it harnesses the talent of a community that's drawn to help solve a problem, whatever it may be. It turns out, Ben learned, that the world has open capacity to work on just about anything. All he needed to do was invite and incentivize the world to solve his particular problem.

Ben did the unthinkable in his industry: he published the company's geological data on the Web for all to see, and challenged the world to do the prospecting. The mining industry was perhaps the most secretive in the world. Going open source with the data was akin to showing his shorts. Industry experts believed a company's main competitive advantage was its ability to locate and mine a vein effectively. Now, Ben was admitting to the world that PMI didn't have a good handle on locating its gold.

The "PMI Challenge" offered a total of $575,000 in prize money to participants who submitted the best methods and estimates. In effect, Ben was trying to create a community of virtual prospectors. Every scrap of information (some 400 megabytes worth) about the 50,000 acre property was revealed on PMI's website. News of the contest spread like a virus on the Internet and more than 1,000 virtual prospectors from 50 countries got busy crunching the data. At about this time, the company geologists mutinied.

FROM YONDER SILO

Within weeks, virtual prospectors were submitting proposals from every corner of the world. There were entries from every form of human life: physicists, math geeks, consultants, military officers, and an army of armchair geologists. Most surprising to Ben, however, were the constructs the participants applied to the mining problem: structures such as computer graphics, calculus, smart systems, and advanced physics were used to support the prospector's positions. Ben began to understand the possible power behind crowdsourcing: contructs that explain one system could be applied to geology, with very interesting results.

The contestants identified 110 targets on the property, more than 80% of which yielded substantial quantities of gold. All told, an amazing 8 million ounces of gold were found — worth well over $3 billion. On just a half million dollar investment.

Ben found his gold; only the veins were housed in a community of virtual prospectors, instead of the ground.

MIDAS MOMENT

BLUEPRINT

In real life, PMI is Goldcorp, a publicly-held company in Canada. Gold-corp has benefitted tremendously from following the crowd. The virtual prospectors brought a host of new ideas to the company, including new drilling techniques, better modeling, and various other useful but unortho-dox methods. This transformed the company from an under-performing $100 million enterprise into a $9 billion juggernaut. Obviously, the share-holders have been big winners here as well.

This book contains numerous stories of how mundane industries have pulled the crowd with great effect. Yet, most companies are still pushing their ideas onto the market, using old methods that are generating old re-sults. I suppose it's counter-intuitive to think that it's possible to leverage intellectual capital by sharing it. Undertandable, since the idea flies in the face of hundreds of years of conventional wisdom.

Crowdsourcing, though, has shown us the edge of innovation: taking constructs that explain one system and applying them to a different system can unleash tremendous creativity. In so many cases, we're seeing that physicists are solving engineering problems; chemists solving biology issues; and mathematicians providing structure to a host of traditionally non-math systems. This "wisdom of crowds" is fully explained in a book by the same name (by James Surowiecki). Surowiecki shows that when faced with the same aggregated data, a crowd of people off the street will almost always make better decisions than a like-kind group of experts in that field. For example, the opening story in his book describes the crowd at a county fair that accurately guessed the weight of an ox when their individual guesses were averaged (the average was closer to the ox's true butchered weight than the estimates of most crowd members, and also closer than any of the separate estimates made by cattle experts). It turns out that experts live in a silo, which prevents them from thinking holistically.

What we're talking about here is mass collaboration on a scale that reflects a connected global economy. The Internet provides the backbone for communities to coalesce around ideas. Look no farther than the development of Linux, the open-source computer operating system, to see how thousands of users can work together for a common good. Knowledge creation now transcends company boundaries. In fact, innovation and creativity are being distributed across firms with the idea that if two heads are better than one, then a million heads should be the goal. But achieving this kind of cooperation requires platforms that harness common interests. In other words, managers need to create compelling value propositions for all stakeholders.

The nature of strategy changes in a pull environment. Instead of depending on resources owned within your company, pulling requires the ability to identify, mobilize, and integrate others' resources to add value for your customers. Each company needs to leverage its intellectual capital and tap others to do what it cannot. In the Aggregation Age, winners play to their strengths but are quick to leverage others' strengths, too.

The following steps can be used to pull the crowd:

Determine how to pull the crowd

Who needs your products or services in order to meet their goals? Answer the question, "What's in It for the Crowd?" This is best determined by asking people what they like, and then aggregating their answer on a community site.

Create a platform that organizes and feeds a niched, networked community of these potential customers

Give them enough value-adding tools — without restrictions — to collaborate and innovate. Make them believe it's in their best interests to contribute something of value to the community.

Collaborate with partners

Leverage your partners' unique intellectual capital to build your platform. Choosing, enticing, and rewarding partners is a key to success in the Aggregation Age.

Dare to share

Innovation within networks occurs when the companies with platforms share capabilities. This is difficult for many business owners because they were taught to shield anything proprietary from outsiders. But in the Aggregation Age, competition is not the central constraint; it's the manager's ability to aggregate value-added solutions.

The lesson for all of us is that the traditional business model is dead. Owning all of your intellectual capital results in too little leverage to create value. Even the conceptual business model is now insufficient, as it doesn't pull the crowd or customer enough to create maximum leverage. Winners today adopt aggregation business models which motivate and incentivize the world to help solve problems, create products and make markets. Where's the bad news in asking others to help you find your gold?

INVESTMENT BANKER MAN

Selling just ain't what it used to be

9

JUST GIVE IT AWAY

ank Fish wasn't getting his due. You see, he owned a small R&D technology company — actually an R&D firm — TechMat, Inc. (TMI). TMI did materials research for the U.S. government, specifically NASA. The government provided monies for applied research, but always wanted more development work from TMI than it was willing to pay for. Thus, Hank constantly felt that his company was missing out on the big money application projects. After a few years, however, Hank noticed, somewhat out of the corner of his eye, an application niche that just might make TechMat a major "D" firm.

A MATERIAL NEED

TMI created a database for the government that contained thousands of material specifications in the field of ceramics. With this database, government engineers could quickly access the properties of specific ceramic materials, thus saving substantial time in material specification and testing. The feedback from the engineers was so good that Hank started wondering if a broader market existed for this service.

Hank looked around the market and saw that no single database contained substantial property data. What's more, the few databases in existence were extremely difficult to use. It almost required a degree in computer science just to query them. Since TMI had already created easy-to-use software to manage a materials database, all it had to do was add the data. Fortunately the company was located in a college town, so resources were available and fairly inexpensive. Hank knew the college library contained references with thousands of material specifications, and that dozens of engineering students would be willing to moonlight and load the database. Within a year, TMI had aggregated the data for several major materials. This amounted to more than 1,000 materials, which Hank believed represented the critical mass necessary to offer the database to the public.

TMI faced two immediate issues. First, it needed to alert the engineering community to its database. Second, it needed to determine how to charge for access. The first problem was solved with a few well-placed advertisements in engineering magazines. The second problem was initially solved by charging users 3 cents to access each materials data sheet. But most engineers only needed to access 2-3 data sheets, so charging 6-9 cents was more hassle than it was worth. Hank realized he needed a different revenue model.

WHAT ABOUT THAT FREE LUNCH?

By the second year, TMI had added several thousand more data sheets to its database. With almost 5,000 searchable records, it was clearly the top database in the industry. Hank had an audacious thought: why couldn't TMI become the Yahoo of the materials industry? Why not charge companies to advertise on its site and let engineers search the site for free? TMI had hundreds of obvious advertiser prospects — namely, the major materials suppliers. They would want to promote their products directly to those who used them. Plus, the more engineers TMI could attract to the site, the more it could charge advertisers. Hank really started appreciating the genius behind the Yahoo model.

It pays to be first. With its first-mover status, TMI attracted the entire materials engineering industry and most of the top tier materials vendors. TMI developed an opt-in capability for its database so it could gather information on its users. To promote branding, TMI sent company pens and other items to first-time users. Originally, it was free to join the site. But Hank correctly believed that when marketing is properly conceived, people would actually pay for the privilege of buying your products or services. So TMI began charging a one-time annual fee for access. A "Silver" registration cost just $100 per year and allowed up to 100 queries each year. A "Gold" registration cost $250 per user and allowed unlimited access. TMI had 20,000 users when it began charging for access. More than 10% of the users paid the annual charge, with 70% of those registering at the Gold level. This change alone added about $500,000 in annual revenue – with no associated increase in expenses. For Hank, it was like found money.

MIDAS MOMENT

TMI incurred relatively little expense to deliver its database. It no longer needed to advertise regularly. The company didn't need any salespeople to contact the materials companies. Hank and one other senior person answered these calls. TMI employed several engineers who reviewed data sheets to make sure they were valid. Students continued to load the data sheets. The sheets themselves were free, as materials companies supplied them as a means of educating the user community. TMI enjoyed annual revenues of several million dollars and employed just five people. Life was good, and it was about to get even better.

WITH JUST A LITTLE IMAGINATION

With more than 20,000 users each day, hundreds of advertisers, and relatively few expenses, the income model was compelling. And Hank was not in the middle of any of it. He worked on the business — not in it. He had created a business model that afforded him time to think, and as he discovered, thinking combined with selective action is where the money is. All of Hank's thinking resulted in a series of "What if's." What if TMI created captive databases for certain companies so they could manage their proprietary materials? What if TMI added value to the data and provided analysis as well as just raw data? What if TMI used its easy-to-use software for other purposes? What if TMI went international? The "what if's" quickly turned into "why not's."

First, Hank went after the low-hanging fruit. From prior conversations he knew there were 8-to-10 companies that needed to better manage their proprietary materials databases. These represented materials and compounds that companies had created through the years but hadn't been properly catalogued. It was fairly easy to get these companies to pay a hefty one-time charge to set-up their databases. Then TMI would charge $30 per material entered, plus charge an annual maintenance fee. Hank figured that TMI incurred less than $10,000 to create the database; less than $10 per record to load it; and less than $5,000 in annual maintenance costs. Of course nearly all of TMI's expenses involved outsourcing to specialist firms or students. All told, the ideas that Hank put into action added hundreds of thousands in profits each year.

Hank also noticed that many companies had downsized their engineering staffs, which made it difficult for them to do basic analysis on materials. So TMI started offering this type of analysis for a fee. Typically, all TMI needed to supply was a sort of the possible materials that would fit the application, plus a recommendation of the best-fit material. TMI hired a few laid-off engineers as independent contractors to provide the analysis, which was reviewed by a TMI employee-engineer before sending it to the client. Within a year, this division was generating more than $250,000 in profits.

MIDAS MOMENT

Hank, now attuned to new opportunities, realized there were many other materials besides those TMI focused on that could be catalogued. He saw that petroleum materials and other liquids needed to be organized. Plus, several major areas such as pharmaceuticals were ripe for TMI's approach. So Hank organized a campaign around each of these areas. He assigned one person to create a game plan – which Hank approved and funded – then that "champion" would oversee the campaign. This method of organizing new areas of business served TMI well.

Finally, materials are an international business, with both regional and large global players and markets. TMI started matching advertising and users by country and region. This made all the sense in the world (literally). When an engineer in the Netherlands searched the database, for instance, he/she would see advertisers that sold materials throughout Europe. TMI needed to add a layer of intelligence to its search model, but it was more than repaid in the ability to sign more advertisers at even better rates.

After 10 years of building a really great company that no longer really needed him, Hank considered how it all started. It wasn't until he began giving away the data sheets that TMI became successful. How instructive. It's another of life's many lessons: most of the time you need to give before you can receive.

BLUEPRINT

In real life, Hank Fish is Henry Bass. Henry's company is Automation Creations, Inc., and the database described above is www.matweb.com. Henry is an American hero, serving his country in Iraq at the time of this writing. Fortunately Henry made the managerial moves described in this story, so his company will continue to prosper while he's away.

There are a number of instructive elements in this chapter. Perhaps the most important is that you must Push before you can Pull. In TMI's case this meant advertising early, plus giving the information away. Once the value proposition to the customers was accepted as compelling, a series of Pull strategies and methods could be deployed. Rarely can you start pulling before you push.

Aggregating a fragmented space is almost always a value-creating activity. There are numerous technology-related examples, such as Google, Microsoft, and Apple. But the Aggregation Age is for all of us, and non-technology spaces need aggregating as well. The last four story chapters of this book give examples of such companies controlling their space.

Leveraging core competencies through scalable business models is always in style. In this chapter, TMI was able to leverage its intellectual capital because it possessed (by design) a scalable model. It required little or no financial capital to grow by a factor of five. This is in direct contrast to old-fashioned models where the baby has to constantly be fed financial capital to grow.

Follow these steps to maximize the "give it away" strategy:

Find your space

There are thousands of spaces that need aggregating. Find yours. Such spaces present themselves, similar to what happened in this story. Be attentive. Try something. Fail and try again.

Aggregate by giving it away

Start with a strategy of giving your value proposition away. At the least, give them a taste for free. It makes for a much less risky purchase later if the customers get a taste for free.

Pull them toward the magnet

If your value proposition is truly compelling, customers will gladly pay for the privilege of buying your stuff. But go slowly on charging for access. Community members must feel that it's a no-brainer to fork over a few hundred bucks for access. It might take a year or so of giving before enough members will not only pay, but will also tell everyone else to do so as well.

Feed them

Your work is only half-done when you gather a community. You must continually feed them with value-creating ideas and action items. Remember that they have other pulls on their time.

Expand the model

If your model is scalable, your main constraint will be your imagination. There will be dozens of ways to grow your business. Plus if you've accomplished Steps 1-4 above, you should have adequate cash flow to give yourself time to think.

Aggregating and controlling your space is a great thing. It's reminiscent of the Robber Barons in the 19th century. Imagine it: you will have created a legal monopoly - but on a black hole niche basis. This is the essence of the Aggregation Age. You can control a niched space as long as your value proposition is stronger than the next guy's. So the choice is yours: either be the Aggregator and create substantial wealth; or be the aggregated and work for a living.

MIDAS MOMENT

10

PULL THE CUSTOMER

A business generates a number of forces that affect its stakeholders and community. Pulling the customer with a compelling value proposition is the single most critical force a company must generate. This contrasts sharply with the pushing force that has characterized business in the past. Historically, business created a product or service, hired a bunch of salespeople, and used them to push the product onto the market. Pushing in this way has typically been very inefficient in terms of timing and cost. Then the Internet changed the rules of buying.

With the Internet, you can post your value proposition for billions to see. This empowers buyers to quickly and cheaply shop all competitors. Since the most compelling proposition ultimately wins, it also pressures companies to constantly sharpen their offerings.

The Aggregation Age has also seen the rise of a new type of marketing help called market makers. Now, the more effective way to organize is to attract and motivate market makers. Market makers are people or organizations that are in position to sell a product or service to large numbers of affinity buyers. In effect, market makers are the new sales people — except market makers aren't on the payroll, and at most, represent a variable expense. Quite often the Maker doesn't require any direct payment at all, because the product or service meets a need of his or her constituents.

Here's a brief summary of the next four chapters.

Chapter 11: The Door Swings In

Most people still push their way into a prospective client's office. This chapter shows how to attract clients so they walk through your door. Lots of clients. This power of attraction can then be institutionalized so that you do not have to attend to each sale. You can then leverage your own activities to a much greater degree. By building a marketing machine, you are in effect cloning yourself — without the baggage of actually having more than one of you around.

Chapter 12: Help Me Sell My Stuff

Imagine you're a schoolteacher and have never managed a business. But you see that certain students are not getting proper instruction, mainly for lack of good teaching materials. What could you do to improve this situation? Read this chapter. The teacher in this story makes several critical, almost fatal, mistakes in starting her business. Fortunately, she finally enlists market makers to help her sell her stuff. This marketing strategy is available to nearly everyone in every industry. All you need to do is ask.

Chapter 13: We've Got You Covered

Attracting individual customers is tricky, mainly because personal tastes vary so much. This situation is exemplified in the world of fashion, where many women want a signature look without paying a signature price. This story shows how an owner created a retailing empire in high-end women's clothes by tapping into the desires of individual customers. Essentially, customers took ownership of the designs, which created a nice pull into the stores. More importantly, it got the cash register singing.

Chapter 14: Death of a Salesman

This chapter is a prequel to a story that appeared in *Midas Managers*. Don Knight is back; this time he's faced with the prospect of eliminating 90% of his salesforce because they're not adding value. This raises an adult question: how do you know if a salesperson is adding value? This chapter tells you how. Traditional salespeople should be very nervous. The Aggregation Age is a marketing age, and therefore is threatening their role. Successful companies set the condition for a sale, and then create a system for insuring that the sale is value-added.

Pulling customers to you is part art, part science. The artful part requires understanding the behavior of players in your space, then crafting a value proposition that truly answers the WIFM question. The science part involves creating a delivery machine that whirls without you. Since the ultimate goal is to leverage you by at least 10:1, you can't have your fingerprints on the machine. I'll let you put your grimy fingers on all the money the machine generates — but only once. Even that activity causes you to temporarily lose leverage. But it sure feels good every once in a while.

MIDAS MOMENT

II

THE DOOR SWINGS IN

Kent Jackson was a typical investment banker. Eager to do well, he would hunt for deals by pushing himself onto the market. He would send out 50 or so letters each week to business owners, follow up most of the letters with a phone call, and invite himself into the owners' lives. Kent always walked through the owners' doors to meet them. Ultimately, a dozen or so opportunities would emerge, with maybe one or two deals closing each year. His approach generated a living, but Kent believed there must be more to life than chasing deals. At the least, he thought, how nice it would be if an occasional owner would walk through his door.

BUT I'M HERE TO HELP

Kent was no dummy. He grew up in a mid-sized family enterprise, so he understood what it meant to own and manage a private business. He also had tremendous credentials, including two advanced degrees, plus a couple of professional designations. Kent had several partners, as well. They were honest, hard-working guys who also felt compelled to help business owners make good decisions about raising capital and transferring their businesses. But after several years of hard charging, the market didn't seem to be listening. It was like pulling teeth to find a good deal.

Why was the market turning a deaf ear? Kent was determined to figure it out, so he spent a lot of time working on an answer to his question. The owners gave him clues. They didn't know anything about finance for private companies (called "private finance"). A few owners had taken corporate finance courses in college, which, at best, is a poor preparation for making financial decisions in a private firm. The owners typically weren't strategic toward their businesses. And they apparently believed they would never sell or transfer their companies. When asked when they planned to exit their firms, they would unilaterally respond, "in about five years." Yet, five years later, the owners would respond in exactly the same way. There didn't seem to be a common ground for having investment banking conversations with business owners.

To make matters worse, some companies in the market were "over-hyping" the values of their businesses. For just $30,000-40,000, an owner would have the privilege of learning that the value of their business was two to three times more than what the market would actually pay for it. An exaggerated value was music to many owners' ears, as they generally believed their businesses were worth far more than market.

THE POWER OF ATTRACTION

Sometime around his fifth year in the industry, Kent drew a line in the sand. He was either going to figure out how to get his door to start swinging in, or he'd find something else to do. He had a few cards to play. He had closed some deals, had a good reputation in the industry, and still had credentials. But how to attract the market? He needed a plan.

When he didn't know exactly what to do, Kent liked to attack on all fronts. His plan: he would write at least one article each month; give at least one talk to a group of business owners every few weeks; and have at least three breakfasts and lunches with other advisors, such as CPAs and lawyers, each week. He had reprints made of all of his articles and he sent them to thousands of prospects. He performed hundreds of selfless acts for the clients of key advisory firms. And business started to trickle in.

Not a bad start, Kent thought, but not exactly the flood of new business he was looking for. He needed to institutionalize his marketing effort. He had to entice the gatekeepers to send traffic his way. The gatekeepers in the private markets are the trusted advisors, such as financial planners, CPAs and lawyers. These are the people with clients, and if they could be incentivized to share their clients, Kent would meet his goals. So Kent approached his best contacts and offered their firms referral agreements. He would pay the firms 20% of the fees he collected if they referred business to him. Plus he would make sure the client stayed with the referring firm after Kent's firm was finished with the assignment.

For several years, this firm referral arrangement worked like a charm. Kent became the go-to investment banker for a handful

MIDAS MOMENT

of CPA and law firms in his city. Simply catering to his referral sources and their clients became almost a full-time job. But it was worth it. After 10 years of struggling in the industry, Kent could finally say "I told you so" to all the doubters (especially within his immediate family).

AND THE DOOR FINALLY SWINGS IN

But why stop with referral agreements with local firms? Why not go regional, and then national? It turns out that writing articles (Kent had written more than 60 at this point) could get you local attention, but it would take a book to crack the national scene. So Kent spent a few years writing a book. Every waking moment was spent on it. Completing the book became a passion for him. Kent learned the secret of authoring a decent-sized book: you had to selfishly give yourself to it. All outside noise had to be silenced, or the book would never be finished. It took four long years, but the tome was finally completed.

Then Kent discovered three more secrets about writing a book. First, few people in his intended audience (business owners) actually read books. They stopped reading about the time they got into business, and correctly sensed that little in the business press would help them create wealth in their private businesses. Second, writing the book is the easy part; getting out on the road and making a market for the book is the challenge. An author needs to spend at least two or three days per week in front of ever-increasing crowds to get a book accepted. Third, the publishers won't really help push the book. Kent signed with one of the largest publishers in the world, thinking they would use their might to make the book successful. Kent's thinking turned out to be strictly the wishful kind. The publisher included the book in just one of its marketing publications (along with 50 other new releases), and this was the high point of their involvement.

So Kent hit the road for a three-year tour. He spoke at meetings of all kinds: trade associations, Rotary Clubs, Chambers of Commerce, etc. He wrote another few dozen articles that all pointed to the book. He put himself out there to be quoted on a fairly wide variety of business topics. After a tour that made Gilligan's stay on the island seem short and well-organized, Kent was ready to go national.

At about the 13-year mark in the industry, Kent was approached by a national bank. Would Kent's firm be interested in becoming the bank's middle market investment banking affiliate? All Kent needed to do was sign a referral agreement. Then another four or five banks called him about the same issue. Then four or five national life insurance and estate planning firms got the idea. The tipping point had been reached. Kent signed more than a dozen national referral agreements in less than a year. Plus he still maintained the local, and a few regional, agreements. More than 50,000 referrors were on the street looking to send their clients to Kent's firm. Let the good times roll.

MIDAS MOMENT

THE BEST LAID PLANS

Then Kent learned another lesson: 50,000 people walking clients through his door was a tad too many for him to service properly. There were days when 50 people would phone or e-mail, all desperately seeking attention for clients who needed more capital yesterday, or might not make payroll on Friday, or had been approached by a major competitor trying to acquire them. By the way, the caller would say, "Would it be too much to ask for Kent to come to Omaha tomorrow?" Yikes!

As a result of this client bull-rush, Kent had to become an investment banking wholesaler. He needed to attract retail investment bankers into his three-ringer who could actually attend to the screaming masses. After six months or so, Kent created a virtual organization that could deal with the market needs. Basically, each referral source had a go-to person in Kent's company, called a financial engineer. All initial contacts were made to these resources, none of whom were Kent's employees (they were independent contractors). The financial engineer would filter out the truly lost, and would quickly engineer solutions for those who could be helped. The engineer would also identify and assign a retail investment banker to handle the engagement if a prospective client became a real client.

Kent has been operating this Cirque du Money for more than five years. It turns out that overnight success really does take 20 years or so to realize. He hears the original doubters tell others that he "fell into something," as if Kent wandered into the pasture of success. All Kent knows for sure is that it takes a lot of work to get the door to finally swing in.

BLUEPRINT

Many of you will recognize that, in real life, I am Kent Jackson. This story fairly summarizes my 20-year journey as an investment banker. The book mentioned in the story is *Private Capital Markets*, also known as my five-pound business card. It actually took me 6,000 hours over a four-year period to write this 250,000-word seminal textbook. But as my teenage daughters have always been quick to point out, "someone smart... could have written it in half the time." This gets no argument from me.

There are a few instructive marketing issues to consider in this chapter. First, pushing services onto an uneducated market is not a maximizing use of time. Some of the smartest people I know are business owners, but they didn't achieve success because of their knowledge of private finance. Schools have done an awful job educating all of us to make good financing and investment decisions in private businesses. Frankly, the academics don't even know there's a difference between managing a large public company and owning a small private firm. Plus, it's little wonder that owners stopped reading business books many moons ago. Why should any owner care how the CEO of IBM or Proctor & Gamble makes decisions? Owners are smart enough to know that none of that should matter to them.

It took me a while to figure it out, but now I know that I should have marketed to business advisors at the beginning. They understood that their clients needed help accessing the private capital markets. Of course, they just don't turn over client lists. All of the intellectual capital-building activities such as articles and books were still required, just to be taken seriously.

Second, it's a good idea to start small when attracting market makers (such as CPAs and lawyers in the story). It takes some time to determine a compelling value proposition to them, and once they bite, it takes time to organize an effective response to their needs.

Third, once you've created the condition for a sale, organize your firm to be able to deal with the masses. I create a virtual, variable structure that spreads financial engineers and dealmakers all over the country. I have little fixed expense, as the workers are paid based on performance. They're all independent contractors, so I don't own any of them. I institute standardized processes and quality control procedures to maintain control. Creating a structure that enables the generation of 50 times more effect than I could achieve on my own is an example of leveraging intellectual capital by 50:1.

Finally, if you're a super-achiever, you need to understand the mathematical principle of "regression to the mean." This simply means that if someone generates an outstanding result, say taking a test, the next time they take a similar test they will score lower. In other words, most people over time tend toward average. And many people will attempt to help you become average like them. They feel threatened by super-achievers. This behavior is almost universally true in larger organizations. The more successful you become, the stronger this pull-to-mediocrity will be. Yet Midas Managers exist and defy regression to the mean. They perform at outlier levels for decades. They are a constant reminder that architecting value-creating propositions never goes out of style.

INVESTMENT BANKER MAN

It hurts more than pride when the door swings out

12

HELP ME SELL MY STUFF

Susan Long had a passion for teaching. She'd been an elementary school teacher for more than 10 years, yet she still felt an adrenaline rush when a child had a light-bulb-on moment. Kids really are our future, and in Susan's mind, the U.S. wasn't doing all it could do to teach the next generation. This was especially true in the case of kids with special needs, such as children with dyslexia, attention-deficit disorder, and bi-polar conditions. Susan believed these kids and others were getting lost in the system, and she aimed to do something about it. She would become an author.

WHERE TO BEGIN?

Susan knew how to teach young kids in a classroom, but she had no idea how to create a series of books and materials that could teach kids when she wasn't there. She had never written a book, nor considered how to create materials that might support a book. How would she ever get a school to adopt her book if she did write it? Further, how does one even get a book published?

First things first. Susan needed to develop a plan. She read a number of books on how to write a business plan. She sought out various successful businesspeople and asked them a thousand questions about starting a business. Finally, she talked with several authors on how to write a book and get it published. After six months she had moonlighted her way into having a business plan.

Her plan called for her company – Special Learning Inc. (SLI) – to create an initial set of three books that would be targeted to 4-to-8-year-olds. This first series would help youngsters learn basic reading skills. As a literary hook, Susan created a couple of cute puppies as constants in the stories. In all the stories, the puppies were owned by a young brother and sister who were the protagonists. Thus the setting for each book was arranged so kids could learn in a fun and empathetic way.

Susan created a book proposal and shopped it to about 50 publishers. The value proposition to the kids was clearly stated and well-researched. However, the value proposition to the publisher wasn't so clear. Strangely enough, publishers are really not in the business of making markets for their books. Instead, they pick authors who will create demand for the book. Essentially, publishers create a book with a pleasing cover and then make it available to the public. But the publishers Susan approached could not see how she would create demand. So after a few months of chasing people who didn't want to be caught, she finally realized that no publisher would take a chance.

So Susan dipped into her life savings and became a publisher. This meant she would need to hire an editor, an artist, and a book printer. Plus, she would need to get her books into the proper channels and create demand to get parents to buy them. Fortunately, there is a community of resources that support self-publishers, so arranging the artisans was purely a matter of money. Susan selected her helpers and they translated her ideas into three great books. The series was off and running.

Getting the books onto bookstores was a totally different matter. Susan found that traditional publishers dominate the big bookstores' shelves, and self-publishers are usually locked out. So Susan started a campaign at her local school system to get her books adopted. Soon, she learned that getting a new series, even if it's just three books, into a school system is just slightly less daunting than putting someone on the moon. There are endless committee meetings and opinions from educators and the public and all of this takes place at least a year before the books would be used – if the minefield can even be entered. And this campaign must be repeated for each school system.

After six months of dealing with politicians, Susan came to an adult realization: she would never sell many books on this path. It was just too hard to create demand. Plus, she had spent most of her savings and had given more books away than she had sold. Other than the satisfaction of having created a cute mini-series, she had little to show.

MIDAS MOMENT

HOW TO MAKE A MARKET

Susan realized that her due diligence had yielded great advice on everything but how to create demand for her books. It turns out that starting a business and creating the books is the easy part. Fortunately in life, when the student is ready, or in this case flat-broke, the master will show. For Susan, this person appeared in the form of Jack Swanson.

Jack was one of those people who had started and grown a series of businesses in many different industries. Jack just looked at things differently than most people. He listened to Susan's history and immediately saw the solution. Susan needed to identify and entice a handful of market makers.

Jack explained to Susan that she could not afford to make a market for her books. It could cost a small fortune to achieve that, and she couldn't sell enough books to justify the investment. Rather, she could use her current resources and inventory of books to meet her goals. All she really needed to do was think in terms of value propositions. In this case, she needed to determine the needs of the groups that could make a market for her value proposition. Who were these groups?

Susan knew the constituencies for her series. These were the kids with special needs, especially kids with dyslexia who needed to be taught differently than most kids. Dyslexia is a disorder of the brain. People with dyslexia need to be taught more directly than others. Susan knew from experience that the earlier kids with dyslexia were diagnosed, the sooner they could be provided with specific, direct instruction on the alphabetic principle. Jack asked: "Why don't you approach the associations that oversee the teaching of students with dyslexia and offer them a holistic set of tools?"

As soon as Jack asked the question, Susan had a moment of clarity: She needed to think smaller. Susan knew that many parents of kids with dyslexia became disenchanted with the school systems' response to their sons' and daughters' special needs; therefore, parents turned to home schooling as a common alternative. Susan now knew what she should do: approach the home schooling association and offer them a compelling value proposition.

AN OFFER THEY CAN'T REFUSE

With just a few phone calls, Susan found her contact – the director of a national home schooling association. She sent the director a copy of the series with a promise that she could customize the books, plus more materials, to the needs of home schoolers. Susan then talked by phone to a number of mothers who were schooling their kids. It became clear that parents would embrace an integrated solution to their kids' needs.

MIDAS MOMENT

It took a handful of meetings with parents, educators, and administrative personnel, but Susan gained valuable insights as to what constituted a total solution to the problem. As a start, Susan learned that research on reading instruction suggests she should re-orient her current materials to provide more direct instruction on the alphabetic principle. More importantly, the constituents told her exactly what they needed for future materials. Parents needed games and other interactive materials to support the learning. Susan learned that reading research suggests multi-sensory instruction may be more effective for kids with dyslexia. Finally, administrators liked the idea that Susan's company would donate 10% of all sales in the program to special needs charities. All stakeholders were on board and incentivized.

A year later, everything had changed for the better. Special Learning Inc. had published three series of books: two were based on reading, one was based on math. The company released board games to support each book, plus had like-kind internet games in production. By working with educators, Susan learned that just a handful of multi-sensory materials were needed to successfully teach the kids. The various stakeholders were SLI's best salespeople. They spread the word around the country, so Susan could mainly focus on executing the marketing plan.

Best of all, other associations were coming to Susan to see if SLI could develop specialized teaching materials to meet their needs. As a teacher, Susan understood the value of learning – and she had certainly learned a great deal while building her business. Perhaps the most important lesson: other people can and will help sell your stuff.

BLUEPRINT

The Aggregation Age is about making markets, mainly niche markets. More specifically, this Age is about pushing your value proposition once, then pulling the market to you. As in physics, the strongest magnet wins.

The story in this chapter is played out every day on Main Street. Most business owners have a strong vision that propels them into starting a business. In Susan's case, she wanted to help special needs kids learn better. But many owners fall short in selecting and implementing strategies, especially marketing strategies. Like Susan, owners get caught up in the "doing" rather than the "what ought to be done." Fortunately for Susan, she found a mentor who understood what Susan should do to be successful. All owner-managers need a mentor.

Prior to the Aggregation Age, businesses built sales forces to push their value propositions. But this is extremely expensive, and often does not pay for itself. Now the more effective way to organize is to attract and motivate market makers. Market makers are people or organizations that are in position to sell a product or service to large numbers. In effect, market makers are the new sales people. Except market makers aren't on the payroll, and at most, represent a variable expense. Quite often, the maker doesn't require any direct payment at all, because the product or service meets a need of his or her constituents.

Another major difference is that salespeople tend to push on a one-off basis. In other words, they sell one customer at a time. This is a 1:1 leverage, which does not promote wealth creation. Contrast this low leverage with attracting a market maker, who may have 1,000 members. Now the leverage is 1,000:1. That is a Midas level of leverage.

To be successful with the marketing strategy in this chapter, do the following.

Clarify your value propositions

It sounds simplistic, but the starting point for every company is knowing what problem they are solving for whom. Then the trick is to provide the solutions in an effective way. If the market is not buying, re-orient your proposition until it does.

Study the market for makers

Almost every value proposition can be distributed through market makers. These are people or organizations that are in position to make a market for your goods or services. In other words, because of who they are, they can bring the market with them.

Motivate and incentivize the makers

Most market makers are not altruistic; they must be motivated and incentivized. It's not unusual for the promoting company to share profits with the maker. But this arrangement is typically on a variable cost basis.

Infiltrate and expand your offerings

Once you have successfully exposed your offerings to a group, listen to what other problems they have, then offer solutions for them as well. The easiest sales occur to existing customers.

Rinse, lather, repeat

If you can play the market maker game once, you can play it across other verticals (customer types) as well. Each vertical is established in much the same way, i.e., follow the steps above to enjoy success. The key is to replicate a successful process.

Midas Marketing sets the condition for a value-added sale. This chapter shows how any product or service can be positioned to be pulled into a vertical. This is a process-intensive activity, with the primary goals of establishing scalability and replicability. But once it is mastered, you can entice other people to sell your stuff, which frees you up to engage in more value-added activities.

MIDAS MOMENT

INVESTMENT BANKER MAN

For fear the employees will figure out what's going on

13

WE'VE GOT YOU COVERED

Sarah Waters had just made the biggest financial mistake of her life. As she pondered whether or not she would survive to fight another day, she vowed to never take another major order from a high-end department store. It was one such store that had just gone bankrupt, owing Sarah's company, All About Designs, more than $300,000. Obviously, supplying women's high-end clothing directly to the stores wasn't working. Sarah needed to change her business model, and the change needed to happen now.

HOW SHE GOT HERE

Sarah had been one of those kids who could draw anything. Her gift eventually grew into a talent for fashion design. By age 25, Sarah had earned a fashion degree and worked four years in the trades for a major design house. On her 26th birthday, she scratched the itch to create her own brand. Thus was born All About Designs.

Sarah had learned a few things in the few years since starting her company. First, she learned how to attract and build a community of freelance design talent. Sarah would create the general look she was after, and then she would send it to 50 or so designers who would create detailed designs. Sarah would choose a handful of designs, and then pitch the buyers at the major high-end clothing stores. At first, All About Designs was all about private labeling.

After a couple of years, Sarah started pitching her own branded line: Sarah Waters. This worked well, but she was still hostage to other companies distributing her clothing.

Sarah also excelled at finding and using small family production facilities around the country that would convert the chosen designs into affordable yet stunning dresses. Local shops provided the initial mock-ups and quick turn clothing needs. But Sarah had suppliers that were 1,000 miles away as well. The Sarah Waters line was too high-end to use production facilities in Asia; it took artisans to create the works. Perhaps only 100 dresses of each pattern would be created. Over time, Sarah learned that certain sewing houses excelled at certain types of patterns, so naturally, she sourced to everyone's strengths. After just a few years she had approved more than 50 facilities, which gave her both flexibility and scalability – all without having to spend money on machines or seamstresses.

Sarah had also become adept at creating design scarcity. She would not flood the stores with endless racks of sizes and options. Too many designs caused the consumer to subconsciously think that the dresses were ubiquitous. Most women wanted an inexpensive, yet expensive-looking, special designer-look with a one-of-a-kind feel. The Sarah Waters line was positioned with those shoppers in mind.

Finally, All About Designs had perhaps the quickest design-to-clothing turnaround in the industry. Sarah referred to this speed as the "Prime Directive." Marsha Waters, Sarah's sister, was a systems nut and created a supply chain software package that morphed into a competitive advantage. Once a store ordered a certain line, All About Design could ship inside one month. This was at least three to four months faster than industry standards. Plus, it enabled stores to special order dresses for events just weeks away, at higher prices. The stores split the higher profit margins generated from the special orders with All About Design.

It was speed-to-market, however, that had caused the big loss. Sarah knew her major customer was having financial problems, but she couldn't resist the largest order in her company's history. Sarah had negotiated a 10-day pay period from the customer, who then filed bankruptcy just one week after taking delivery of the dresses. All About Design used the balance of its credit line to pay its suppliers, a move that caused a severe cash crunch, but earned Sarah fierce loyalty from her vendors.

A NEW BEGINNING

Sarah took stock of her situation. It was just bad enough to force major changes in the way she operated. She needed to find a way to leverage her company's core strengths, while creating a different path to market. Sarah Waters was about to go retail.

MIDAS MOMENT

Sarah didn't know the retail business, which it turns out, was a good thing. Traditional retail in high-end fashion was predicated on estimating fashions 6-to-9 months out, and was mainly driven by fashion shows in Paris. So the entire industry was built on guessing what would be fashionable in the future. Of course, this could cause major financial pain if a season was lost due to poor estimation. At the least, most current fashions were ultimately discounted by more than 50% to reflect changing buyer attitudes over time.

The Sarah Waters retail chain was launched on a Wednesday, mainly because it took longer for the store fixtures to arrive than anyone thought possible. In any event, Sarah chose a Mall location because of the conventional wisdom that high-end dress buying occurred in high-end Malls. But that was the last anyone saw of conventional wisdom in a Sarah Waters store.

Sarah did the unthinkable in fashion design: her store sported all new designs every month. Goodbye Paris, Hello Americana. It was as if a Sarah Waters store was reborn each month. The store would celebrate the arrival of the new designs with a "Fashionably New" party. Customers were invited to view the new designs as models walked down a make-shift runway. Eventually, the runway was moved into the main part of the Mall, so hundreds of people could see the new designs. To sell remainder inventory, each store ran an end of the month event called a "Sarah's Closet" sale. No special orders were allowed during these last three days, and customers were told throughout the month not to expect many size or design options. In other words, the store managers created a sense of enforced scarcity throughout the month, and selling out became a self-fulfilling prophecy.

DESIGN HOUDINI

There's a reason why no other fashion design store in the world rotated its inventory each month: it couldn't be done! But somehow it happened at the 16 Sarah Waters stores (she added another 15 stores in her second year of retail). The combination of the Prime Directive, flexible production outsourcing, and the company's logistical systems enabled Sarah Waters to pull off this monthly magic act.

As with most important business activities, new designs started with customer desires. Each month, store managers fed every nuance of customer behavior back to the company designers. This communication involved more than just reporting item sales. Managers and salespeople of each store engaged their customers to find out why they bought what they did, as well as what they wanted but couldn't find. Sarah created an intra-net that allowed store personnel to explain what they were hearing directly to the designers. Plus each Friday afternoon, there was a conference call between designers and store managers.

MIDAS MOMENT

Designers would take the information they collected (including actual sales) and spend the first weekend of each month creating new designs. Within days, these designs were e-mailed to appropriate vendors in the supply network. Suppliers understood that they had two weeks to convert the designs into the plethora of sizes and shapes required. It then took another week to get the new dresses into the stores. These monthly rituals became institutionalized, with machine-like effectiveness.

Some unexpected magic resulted from the soul of the machine. Current customers not only came to the stores the first weekend of each month, but they also brought their friends, who brought their friends. Afterward, blogs and websites were created by the community (not the company) to highlight new designs and to simply discuss the coolness of the model. The unexpected result was that customers began to understand their roles in the process: they engaged store personnel to make sure that their voices were heard for future designs. In effect, customers now owned the designs. Thus, they felt they owned the store.

As Sarah witnessed the evolution of her little dress shop into an empire of more than 100 stores, she couldn't help but wax poetic. She had set out to bring high design to the masses, in an affordable, timely and comfortable environment. What resulted was that the masses really brought the designs; she just covered them with their own desires.

BLUEPRINT

This story is loosely based on the Zara stores, founded in 1975 by Amancio Ortega. Zara is the flagship chain store of Inditex Group in Spain. It is claimed that Zara needs just two weeks to develop a new product and get it to stores, compared with a six-month industry average, and launches around 10,000 new designs each year. Zara has resisted the industry-wide trend towards transferring production to low-cost countries. Perhaps its most unusual strategy is its policy of zero advertising; the company prefers to invest a percentage of revenues in opening new stores instead.

Zara is a vertically integrated retailer. It designs, produces, and distributes itself. Unlike similar apparel retailers in the same market, Zara controls most of the steps on the supply chain. Fifty percent of the products Zara sells are manufactured in Spain, 26% in the rest of Europe, and 24% in Asian countries and the rest of the world. So while competitors outsource production to Asia, Zara makes its most fashionable items -- half of all its merchandise -- at a dozen company-owned factories in Spain, using mostly Galician cheap labor. Clothes with a longer shelf life, such as basic tee-shirts, are outsourced to low-cost suppliers, mainly in Asia and Turkey.

The keys to the story in this chapter are:

- Short lead times which leads to more fashionable clothes

- Lower quantities which lead to scarce supply

- More styles which lead to more choices and a greater likelihood of finding the right mix

- Create the machine that converts design into clothing at warp speed

- Control of the supply chain enables everything to happen

These key elements are so Aggregation Age. The main point is to follow the lead of your customers to the point where they take ownership of your program. Build a machine that institutionalizes your conversion process, which enables maximum leverage. Then control your space so you can minimize time to market. Then follow the directions on the back of a Head & Shoulders bottle: lather, rinse, repeat.

The "control your space" strategy can be copied by following these steps:

Design the machine

Marketing machines do not create themselves: they must first be designed. The value architecture used in this chapter can be replicated in most other businesses. Sarah knew where she wanted to go with the business, and this destination of "warp turnover of clothing designs" not only became the company's mantra; it also dictated the design of the company. Knowing the destination is far more important than knowing the explanations of how you'll get there. The "how" will reveal itself. The "where" is strategic and must be determined upfront by the key manager(s).

Create the machine

Once you know your destination and have your business model designed, you need to build the machine. This is typically accomplished by building core competencies in the company, then linking them together to form an effective process chain. Managing the steps will almost always require use of a cutting edge computer system.

Control your space

It's no longer enough to just control your process chain (that's so Conceptual Age); now you must reach higher and control your space. This involves controlling the process flow in and around your company, such as vendors, outside resources, and even customers. Controlling one's space used to be the province of large companies only. However, in the Aggregation Age it's essential for all successful companies to do so.

MIDAS MOMENT

Engage and empower the customer

The simplest way to know what a customer thinks and wants is to ask them. But this needs to be done in an organized fashion, so that information is collected and used in a maximizing way. It's not enough just to engage the prospective and current customer base, either. They must be empowered to make decisions about your products and services. Of course this can be a slippery slope. It is management's job to aggregate the data so that not just one customer's voice is heard above the masses.

Create a feedback loop

Management needs to collect customer information quickly and act on it immediately. We live in an attention deficit disordered society, so time is of the essence. The feedback loop of customer desires should be measured in days – not weeks.

In the Aggregation Age, conversion speed is vital. Change is now geometric, so our responses to market needs and desires must move beyond the "we'll get to it eventually" mentality. Predicting success in this Age is easy: whichever company designs the most compelling value proposition and packages it most effectively wins. And this secret sauce of the Midas recipe is actually free and available to everyone, and is always in fashion.

INVESTMENT BANKER MAN

Getting the most out of a sales force

14

DEATH OF A SALESMAN

D on Knight walked into the rectangular conference room at Automated, Inc. with a purpose — an unfortunate purpose at that. To save Automated, Don needed to fire 12 salespeople. In fact, by noon, Automated would be down to only one salesperson. As Don strode to the front of the tension-filled room, he wondered if his new plan for generating sales for his mid-sized company would actually work.

A NEW BEGINNING

Don was a newcomer to the ranks of business owners. His career had been spent advising owners in capital raises and transfers. But, like so many investment bankers, Don thought he had what it took to jump to the other side of the table. From a fraternity brother, Don learned that a Fortune 500 company had decided to divest a number of non-core divisions, including one located in his town. The division, Automated Inc., distributed vision and motion controls used to automate industrial activities. For several years, it had been breaking even on about $10 million in annual revenue. While it had no proprietary products, it had some geographic protection for several of its product lines. But when the parent had tried to sell Automated via a standard Wall Street auction, there were no takers. So Don scraped some money together, borrowed more, and acquired Automated.

Don should have known that no matter how much he studied a company or its industry, he wouldn't really be able to grasp the opportunity until he owned it. Unfortunately, by then it would be too late, since he would be stuck with the investment. This is what happened with Automated. During the year before the sale, the parent company had cut off support for the division, and several key employees had quit. The market had softened, and globalization was pushing the industry overseas, putting the hurt on domestic suppliers.

During the first four months Don owned Automated, the company lost $50,000 per month. That cut its cash on hand by two-thirds, to just $100,000 (it had cost $100,000 to close the transaction, leaving starting working capital of $300,000). Don was feeling the heat. So he did what all first-time owners do: he cut his staff.

Releasing eight of his 50 employees lessened the monthly losses, but didn't solve the ultimate problem. Profit margins on a number of products were declining. Items such as programmable logic controllers were becoming commodities, and many of Automated's other products could be ordered off the Internet for much less from Don's competitors. Yet Automated didn't even have a website.

And in a period of soft sales, Automated hemorrhaged cash. There was a sales manager, 13 outside salespeople (supported by five sales coordinators) and four inside salespeople. There were five engineers with substantial product knowledge, and a sizeable clerical staff. Everyone was on salary and the salespeople also got bonuses based on the total gross margin dollars earned on the products they sold.

To survive and eventually create value, Don needed to move Automated away from its push marketing model. As a project engineering company, it was similar to a machine shop or a contractor. That is, it had no recurring revenue stream. Don needed to reconceptualize the entire marketing model.

A REALLY NEW BEGINNING

After several months at the helm, Don knew Automated was in danger of going out of business. He was almost personally tapped out. He had to take drastic steps, well beyond the cut-around-the-edges stuff he'd been doing. He suspected that his bakers-dozen salesforce was not value-added. Each month the sales meetings were full of stories of how major projects were about to be released, but little seemed to come Automated's way. Don decided to put all salespeople on a monitoring system that would show if they were adding value to the company.

Don worked with his sales manager and created a new compensation plan for salespeople, to be effective January 1. This plan would pay more to salespeople who had added value, but it would drastically cut the compensation of the story tellers. Here's a summary of the plan.

MIDAS MOMENT

SALES COMPENSATION PLAN
Characteristics of Compensation Plan

- **Transparent and Understandable.**
  Everyone needs to understand the Plan.

- **Cumulative.** Compensation is based on
  cumulative annual totals beginning January
  1 of each year (to avoid income bunching
  in a month).

- **Net Income.** Employee receives 50% of
  Net Income produced by the Employee.

- **Risk Return.** Return of 25% return on risk
  to owner.

- **Data.** Data from the immediate prior month
  shall be used to compute compensation for
  current month.

- **Salary Date.** 15th of each month; one time
  per month.

- **Preparation.** Data from the immediately
  preceding month is used to avoid month
  end crunch.

COMPENSATION FORMULA FOR EACH EMPLOYEE

Gross Income By Employee

Less: Direct Employee Expenses

Less: Overhead Per Employee

Less: Risk Return

   = Net Income By Employee

   x 50%

   = Compensation to Employee

    (but not less than Guaranteed Salary)

DEFINITIONS

Employees. Full time employees in the physical Local Office.

Direct Employee Expenses. Expenses directly related to the employee, for example, health insurance, disability insurance, retirement contributions, continuing education, seminars, and entertainment expenses, excluding Salary of Employee.

MIDAS MOMENT

Guaranteed Salary. Monthly Salary of Employee guaranteed by Local Office.

Gross Income By Employee. All income received from the efforts of the employee as reflected in the Receipt Allocation Report.

Central Office. Automated, Inc.

Overhead Per Employee. All overhead expenses of Central Office less all Salary, all Direct Employee Expenses and dividends to owner. The owner of the Central Office determines the composition of overhead expenses. Employees are encouraged to reduce overhead, benefiting all.

Receipt Allocation Report. Produced in Time Matters software, and objectively allocates the income received to the persons recording time at applicable rates. This is used to calculate Gross Income By Employee.

Risk Return. Guaranteed Salary, Direct Employee Expenses and Per Employee Overhead times 25%.

Salary. Compensation of the Employee, including Guaranteed Salary and nonguaranteed Salary.

This plan measured whether salespeople were covering their monthly expenses, plus whether they were generating a fair return to the shareholder. Expenses included direct and indirect costs, such as proper allocation of company resources. Don felt he should achieve at least a 25% return on his investment.

Viewing investment and return in this holistic way solved several major problems for Don:

- He could now determine the return-on-investment for each salesperson.

- He could develop compensation schemes for salespeople around return targets.

- Salespeople would have an incentive to police and minimize non-productive expenses.

MIDAS MOMENT

- Salespeople would become part of the marketing effort because they would know their "investment nut."

- Those who did not meet the return on investment goals would not be surprised (at least in theory) when they were replaced.

- Don could manage his goal of meeting a certain return on his investment in the firm all the way down at the individual employee level.

The Sales Manager created a simple spreadsheet for each salesperson so they could easily see how much it cost each month to support and pay them, as well as how they were doing each month. Every month, the Sales Manager would meet with each salesperson to review results, which were also posted for all to see at the monthly sales meetings. By the end of the third month, it was clear to everyone that only one salesperson was contributing value. Notably, this person was taking home more than $30,000 per month. No other salesperson was covering his or her expense allocation, let alone generating a 25% return on investment.

AN END TO THE REALLY NEW BEGINNING

After three months, Don had seen enough. It was clear that a dozen salespeople would never cover their monthly nuts. He needed to totally reconceptualize the company's marketing and sales effort. But before he eliminated 12/13 of the sales problem, he would create a marketing machine. Since the one-off sales approach was not going to work, he would convert Automated into a branded products company.

Step one was to take stock of the intellectual capital, or know-how, that existed inside Automated. Leveraging that resource would be the basis for reconceptualizing the model. Of course, Don had never worked in the controls industry, so he didn't know exactly what Automated had. But after dozens of conversations with engineers and salespeople, he determined that the company housed substantial know-how. Automated's core competencies included the ability to integrate components into a turnkey solution, especially when wireless transmission and remote control were involved. Automated had completed a number of interesting engineering projects through the years, which included:

MIDAS MOMENT

- A bar code tunnel for managing inventory in
  a plant.

- A controller for managing activities in
  a greenhouse, including lighting and
  watering.

- A system that uses wireless networks to
  control nearly every machine in a factory.

After hearing about numerous successful engineering projects,
Don picked one and packaged it. Then Automated could sell the
wheel, instead of constantly reinventing it. Within two years, Automated had converted entirely to a branded products company. But
that is another story.

BLUEPRINT

True Midas-ites will recognize this story is a prequel to Chapter 16, "Productize or Die!" from *Midas Managers*. The Productize chapter describes how Don Knight converted Automated into a branded products company. This current chapter shows how he came to the conclusion that he needed to.

The Aggregation Age is a marketing age, and therefore is threatening the role of traditional salespeople. Pushing the service or product to the customer is no longer efficient or effective. Successful companies set the condition for a sale, and then create a system for insuring that the sale is value-added.

In this chapter Don Knight creates a new compensation plan for salespeople, the basic gist of which is to identify and properly allocate expenses to each salesperson. This can be a little tricky, and more than a little political. For guidance on these issues, I refer you to Chapter 21, "The Value of Investment," in *Midas Managers*. Don also needs to receive a fair return on his investment, which he decided was 25%. Every owner needs to determine an appropriate return based on the risk of owning a particular business. Early stage companies typically have substantial risk of ownership, therefore a fairly high return is required, say 50%. Large companies normally are less risky, and require a return in the 10-20% range.

The following steps can be used to implement the "sales value creation" strategy:

Include salespeople in the compensation plan discussion

Let them know the reason you're making a change. Make them responsible for their own expenses and give them a say in what expenses are to be allocated to them. Ultimately, they must take ownership of this plan to have any chance of success. It's best to start the new program on January.

Allow salespeople to see how everyone else is performing

Many of the salespeople will share allocated expenses, so they need to see how certain indirect expenses are allocated. Give salespeople some power in making changes to the team. For instance, if an internal sales coordinator is not fully supporting the salespeople, give them the power to bring in someone new.

Review monthly plan reports with each salesperson

If a particular salesperson is not creating value, work with them to change this outcome. You'll see that "A" players love the new scoring system, whereas "C" players hate it. Most business value is created by the "A" team.

Make the hard decision

At some point it may become clear that some salespeople will never create value for the firm. It should be obvious to them first, if they understand the new system at all. Owners must decide for themselves an appropriate period of under-performance before taking action. In exponentially changing times, six months is forever.

It's about marketing

Ultimately, you want to convert your company to a marketing, not selling, firm. Follow the other chapters in this book to find a strategy that best fits your appetite and circumstances. This chapter can be viewed as an incremental way of getting there.

As Don Knight found out, a business owner's ultimate respon-sibility is to create a condition where the day-to-day success of the company doesn't depend on him or her. Converting from a selling to a market-driven business is a good start. Only the owner can position the business to sell the wheel again and again.

MIDAS MOMENT

INVESTMENT BANKER MAN

Enforced scarcity of the mind

15

AGGREGATE YOUR SPACE

"Control your space" is the mantra of the Aggregation Age. It's too expensive to own your sphere of influence, plus it's not an efficient use of time or capital, even if you could afford it. As opposed to the Conceptual Age, when it was important to control your process chain, the Aggregation Age requires higher-level thinking and participation. Now you need to control your space.

Value architecture is at a premium in the Aggregation Age. This is the ability to design and execute value-added solutions in space. This tends to be a right brain-led activity, which explains why creative thinking is the most critical talent required. Financial capital is not a constraint for a well-architected plan. Given all these circumstances, it follows that tremendous wealth can be created quickly in the Aggregation Age.

Fortunately, there are many ways to control your space, as the following Chapter summaries indicate.

Chapter 16: Take My Business – Please!

Perhaps the easiest way to grow in tough economic times is to just absorb the weak hands. Thousands of companies will fall on hard times in the next few years. There's a time-honored capitalistic tradition of creating wealth based on other people's misfortune. This chapter is a continuation of the Consolidation Math Game story from *Midas Managers*. It shows that in terrible economic times, instead of acquiring companies to grow, you can achieve the same result by simply accepting what the market will give you.

Chapter 17: Bundle It With Joy

It's now possible to make major land grabs in your supply chain. Basically, in the Aggregation Age we all need to become "space integrators." This chapter shows how one company converts from a discrete parts supplier to a modular aggregator. The strategy cost the aggregator almost nothing to implement. But it takes some creativity and salesmanship to convince a customer that it's in his or her company's interest to allow another company to consolidate part of its supply base.

Chapter 18: A Global Niche-aholic

It's a global economy — why not exploit niches on a worldwide basis? It's something of a paradox that small niches are so readily available in such a big world. But behavior is different in different cultures, and managers need to adapt and become flexible in their thinking. Beyond having a compelling value proposition, perhaps the most important skill is to choose partners and country managers who add value to your proposition.

Chapter 19: Creating a Virtuous Cycle

This capstone story describes a major initiative I have launched around the country. Our goal is nothing less than to reconceptualize how private business is conducted in the U.S. To accomplish such a large task, we've engaged major universities in the effort. In effect, we're educating and interning students in mid-sized companies that are coached by Midas Mentors. These Mentors typically are alumni of the university. A virtuous cycle will result: the students will become the next generation of successful business owners, and current Mentorees will become the next generation of Mentors.

The stakes are high in the Aggregation Age. People who aggregate their space will leverage their intellectual capital to a high degree, and thus create substantial wealth. People who fail to aggregate will be aggregated, and will earn a living, possibly a lifestyle. It's a personal choice that everyone will make — whether they know it or not.

MIDAS MOMENT

16

TAKE MY BUSINESS – PLEASE!

om Rudolph had seemingly done the impossible. With little of his own money invested, he had consolidated a couple of dozen companies into a $350 million in sales juggernaut. Then, he sold out to a public company for almost $200 million. Life was good — for a while.

A person like Tom needs a constant challenge. Getting his golf handicap under 10 took almost a year. Then charity work took another year. Then boredom pervaded his very soul. Just about the time he was searching for a high bridge, though, opportunity knocked. And it came in a familiar form.

OPPORTUNITY IS ON LINE 2

One of Tom's old managers was on the phone, telling him that Tom's old company was cratering. The public Giant that had overpaid for it just a few years earlier was now itself teetering on the edge of bankruptcy. Tom could only imagine the cacophony of blame that must have been ricocheting around corporate headquarters. Many in the industry had started pools to bet on which day and month the company would fold. The question before Tom: would he be interested in buying back his old company?

Tom was reluctant. He had hyper-built Corrugated Acquisition Company, since renamed Corrugated Specialties, in a way that didn't exactly cause deep emotional attachment. For him, it was just an investment that went well, so Tom couldn't see himself as the cavalry coming over the hill. But, on the other hand, Tom still had a nose for investment opportunities, and for the right price, he might be interested. Tom told his ex-manager to let the parent know that he might be interested in buying the division.

A few weeks went by before Tom heard anything. He was working a soft draw on the range one day when his cell rang. It was Jerry Putnam, CFO of the faltering Giant, whom Tom knew from the negotiations. After the normal pleasantries, Jerry said that the Giant had been able to secure new financing, and reports of its demise had clearly been exaggerated. This news cost Tom money, since he had entered the death pool, but he didn't mention it. In any event, Jerry explained that the Giant had decided to divest Corrugated Specialties, and if Tom was interested in taking a look, Jerry would have the investment banker call him.

Like most successful business owners, Tom disliked Wall Street investment bankers. They wore high-priced MBAs and smelled of unearned self-righteousness. Tom even believed that if you shot them all, American business would probably be better off. So when the young banker phoned a few days later, Tom thanked him for the call but indicated he had thought about the opportunity, and would pass. The young banker almost broke down, pleading with Tom to reconsider, declaring what a wonderful deal this could be for Tom; how he could darn near steal the company. This banker, of course, was being paid by the Giant to get the maximum price in the market. Tom once again considered the mass shooting idea, but decided to leave it be for now.

HITHER YONDER AUCTION

Tom would never participate as a buyer in an auction. But that's what the young banker was offering Tom, a chance to join the rest of the cattle in an auction in which the slaughter was the privilege of overpaying for the business. No thank you. First, Tom had all the money in the world. With this much money, he could afford to have the patience of Job. Second, the economy was starting to tank, so Tom knew that most investors would be scrambling to their fox holes. Third, Tom had no emotional attachment to Corrugated, so he really didn't care if he bought the company. Yes, it was time to visit Hawaii — for three months.

Much as Tom suspected, the auction was a bust. It usually takes a few months before it becomes clear whether an auction will work or not. With the sale of Corrugated, it was definitely a "not." Tom learned of the busted auction from his ex-manager. Upon hearing the news, Tom let slip that he had been contacted by the owner of Corrugated's death competitor, inquiring if Tom would be interested in buying it. Things were certainly getting interesting. Yes — it was definitely time to spend a month in Europe.

MIDAS MOMENT

At some point between Tom's time in Paris and Marseilles, the Giant had fired the Wall Street investment banking firm. The CFO left Tom a few voice mails and a couple of emails. Finally, Tom responded that he was in Europe and would be home in a couple of weeks, at which point he would be in a position to talk.

Tom eventually called the CFO and arranged to meet for lunch. The CFO tried to play it cool, but it was clear that he had been charged with the divestiture of Corrugated. With no buyers still active from the auction, Jerry asked if Tom had an interest in buying the division. Tom had about 20 minutes of reasons prepared why he had no interest. He could see the life draining from the CFO. So finally, Tom threw him a lifeline, saying he would consider buying the division if the price was right. Tom thought he could see blood returning to the CFO's face. They left the lunch agreeing that the CFO would create a document containing terms he believed the Giant's board of directors would accept. Tom agreed on this course of action, and then casually mentioned that he hadn't been to the Far East in quite some time.

MUCH ADO ABOUT NOTHING

Tom was underwhelmed when he finally saw the term sheet. It was as if the Giant had not learned anything from the unattended auction. Yes — it was definitely time to head to China.

A month or so later, Tom finally returned to the United States. All the travel had actually tired him, but at least his blood pressure was constant. The same could not be said for the Giant. They had somehow learned that Tom was almost ready to acquire their death competitor. This would be a disaster, for then it would put Tom back in the industry, plus insure that he would no longer buy Corrugated. So the CFO called once again – this time asking what Tom would pay for Corrugated. Tom said $50 million, on a debt-free basis, of course (meaning the Giant would deliver Corrugated to Tom without any interest-bearing debt on the balance sheet). The CFO, understandably nervous, said they had bought the company from Tom just a few years before for $200 million! How could he take a $50 million offer to the board? Tom asked if the CFO had any other offers to submit to the board. When the CFO didn't answer, Tom had his answer.

It took another 60 days of wrangling, lawyering, hollering, and a bunch of other "ing" words before Tom finally owned Corrugated Specialties again. He actually acquired it for $40 million, because he had inserted a purchase price adjustment clause into the contract. When all of the dust settled, the clause had saved Tom $10 million. Not that this money came out of Tom's pocket. He had arranged to borrow the entire amount anyway, keeping his powder dry for a rainy day.

MIDAS MOMENT

START BUILDING THE ARK

And it was pouring rain in the markets. When the economy hits the skids, packaging companies feel it first and worst. Corrugated was no different. Every financial metric was down, and the rabbit hole looked quite deep. Of course, Tom had known this was coming. That's why he paid less than net asset value for the company. But now he needed to move away from financial engineering and into value creation mode. Basically, he needed to grow Corrugated by using the same strategy he had just used with the Giant — except the sellers would be smaller companies. In other words, he needed to absorb the weak hands.

It's always the same in each recession. Companies that go into the downturn unprepared don't come out alive. Too much debt, too much customer concentration, too high a fixed overhead will take a company out when the demand curve falls. This is a period when most people lose their heads. They do the exact opposite of what will grow their business: they stop all marketing; fire their salespeople; and try to wait out the storm. The problem with this approach is that the economic storm may rage for years. After six to nine months of hunkering down, the only thing that's really changed for the unprepared is that their cash flow is no longer large enough to keep them in business. And that is what Tom was counting on.

In this way, Tom was "old school." He learned many years before that you often make more money taking advantage of other companies' mistakes than you can by leveraging your own triumphs. And many companies in the packaging industry had made a ton of mistakes.

Tom put out the word (meaning he told just one of his salespeople) that Corrugated would help out distressed business owners. By "help," he meant — although he may not have clearly stated it — that Corrugated would take the failing business off their hands for net asset value, but that the owner would have a chance to get whole again by working for Corrugated. If this sounds like the Consolidation Math game all over again, it was; except that by absorbing weak hands, Tom had little money in each acquisition. As before, Corrugated merged the acquired businesses into its own, saved money on redundant expense structures, and picked up new sales. Corrugated absorbed five weak hands the first year, and four more during the second year. These acquisitions added about 40% more sales to his company, but more importantly, more than doubled Corrugated's earnings.

So Tom is riding out the storm, getting ready to cash-in once again. Who knows, thought Tom, maybe the Giant will pay him more than $200 million for the company again.

MIDAS MOMENT

BLUEPRINT

Tom Rudolph knows how to buy low and sell high. It really isn't as hard as most people make it out to be. You just need to understand the private capital market transfer cycle. It's long been held that investors cannot time investments in the public stock markets. This is correct. However, timing the private capital markets can be accomplished — especially as it relates to buying or selling a private business.

The U.S. private capital markets follow a 10-year transfer cycle, as illustrated by the chart below.

Ten Year Transfer Cycle

	Deal Recession (Buyer's Market)	Prime Selling Time (Seller's Market)	Almost Recession (Neutral Market)	
1980	1983	1988	1990
1990	1993	1998	2000
2000	2003	2008	2010

As you might expect, the transfer cycle follows the U.S. economy. The first few years of every decade finds the economy either in recession, or in a serious slow-down. In either event, senior lenders decide to severely restrict their lending activities. The 4th year of the past few decades has been a transition year: profits build in the system and people start looking forward again.

The private markets are open for business from years five through eight of the decade. During this period, capital flows freely, profits increase in most industries, acquisition multiples are at their zenith, and we all get busy over-building and over-leveraging. Such excesses eventually cause storm clouds to form — which firmly take hold by the end of the decade. Consider where we are in the cycle and the recent sub-prime meltdown: this may be the catalyst that causes senior lenders to restrict credit in the system, which would initiate the next capitalistic reset (aka recession … depression).

It's not all bad news, though. Substantial wealth can be created by acting on this transfer cycle. For instance, buying businesses during the recessionary periods, and then selling them during the go-go years is usually a winning strategy. What's stopping more people from playing this game? The answer depends on who they are. Most private business owners are emotionally tied to their businesses, so buying and selling their firms is not something they do routinely. Most private equity groups, on the other hand, do not synchronize their activities with the transfer cycle. They tend to raise capital and acquire during the high water periods — which may force them to hold their investments longer than they would like (or sell at a loss).

For the record, as the story above shows, any business can be sold at any time during the 10-year cycle. What we're talking

MIDAS MOMENT

about here is maximizing the sale. Selling-out during a period of
low profitability and low acquisition multiples does not typically
generate a satisfied seller.

Follow these steps to play the "Take My Business — Please!"
game:

Respect the transfer cycle

It is what it is. Ignore it at your own peril.

Get in position

This strategy requires ownership of a platform company with available systems and management capacity and key managers who are
experienced in handling hyper-growth. If you don't have a scalable
platform, use this strategy to acquire just one or two companies.

Strike while the iron is hot

When you're ready, put the word out to attract companies in trouble. Don't be afraid to acquire companies out of bankruptcy. This
strategy works best where add-on companies can be identified and
purchased within a fairly short period of time. Contract with owners
to keep them involved after you acquire their companies through
the use of employment agreements, seller notes, earn-outs, or some
combination of the three.

Don't fall in love with the result

Timing is important here. This strategy works best when it is initiated at the tail end of a recession and completed with a sale of the
platform company within five years.

Successfully playing this game relies on having substantial experience in your industry, a strong team to help you raise capital and identify potential acquisitions, and the ability to integrate multiple companies into your platform. But if you've got the vision and courage to try, tremendous wealth should be just around the corner.

MIDAS MOMENT

17

BUNDLE IT WITH JOY

When we last visited Terry Lancaster, manager of Super Films, he had just acquired the company from a corporate parent that was more interested in getting the division off its balance sheet than growing it. So Terry had successfully played the Corporate MBO game. Now he faced an entirely different problem: he needed to grow the business to the next level.

THE BUSINESS

Terry knew his business and industry: he had spent nearly 20 years toiling in the engineering and sales ranks before being promoted to general manager of Super Films, a manufacturer of specialty acrylic films. These films were used for a variety of purposes, but most of its parts ended as the finish on cars. Super's films were offered in virtually any color requested by the OEM; in fact, the Company's claim to fame was that they could match the entire color spectrum. In essence, Super Films' product was the last layer of color that showed on the outside of certain parts on cars, such as body side moldings and fascias.

Super Films' main competitors were companies that spray-painted parts. Typically these companies also made the parts they painted, such as plastics manufacturers. Films were usually more expensive than comparable spray-painted parts, mainly because the plastics companies viewed painting parts as a loss leader; they made most of their money on the base part. So Terry faced a market dilemma: how can you win against a group that was willing to break even or lose money on the competing product? His answer: change the rules.

Terry needed to change the rules to better control his space. Super Films supplied a single part that was highly visible on expensive vehicles. This raised several issues. First, Super Films wasn't the only company in the world that could supply the parts in question. Thus it could be shopped by the customer, which effectively held profit margins in check. Second, since Super's films provided Class "A" surface finishes that totally covered the substrate, it was in the customer's best interest to use as inexpensive a substrate as possible. Since Super did not control the choice of materials its product covered, and the underlying manufacturer wasn't usually incentivized to move to cheaper materials, the customer was often paying too much for the substrate. Finally, even though Super's part was visible, it could be hurt by the manufacturers who applied the film onto their parts. At times, either the film wasn't glued correctly or was damaged in the application. In both cases, it came back to haunt Super.

A MODULAR VIEW

Terry thought about these problems and saw opportunity. What if Super went to its customers and offered to supply the module that contained its part, rather than just supply a single part? In other words, rather than have 15-20 suppliers each sending the customer individual parts, what if Super Films bundled all of these parts into a single module?

Terry thought the offer might be appealing to several customers, as the customers were trying to outsource many of their assembly operations. It wasn't a good use of resources for customers to be in the sub-assembly business. Sure, the car companies needed to ultimately assemble the vehicle, but it made economic sense for them to assemble modules rather than individual parts. The issue for the car companies was to correctly choose and incentivize someone to assemble the modules.

However, not all of the car companies shared this view. Terry learned early that American car companies still had a command-and-control view of business. Incontrovertible evidence to the contrary, the Big 3 thought they needed to own the entire assembly process. Plus, they preferred to keep their assembly plants working — so they had deaf ears when it came to an outside vendor assembling modules for them. Japanese car companies, on the other hand, viewed vendors as partners and welcomed the idea that cost could be taken out of the modules by outsourcing — and perhaps quality could be improved at the same time.

MIDAS MOMENT

Two of the Japanese car companies accepted Terry's offer, although on a limited test basis. Basically, Super Films became a Tier 1 supplier, with total responsibility to supply several small modules. In each module, Super was supplying less than $1 million per year in their films. But each module in total represented a dozen or so parts, with combined sales of more than $100 million per module. Terry and his team worked with the car companies to determine pricing per module, but his goal was to cut the expense by at least 10%. This goal was in alignment with the car companies; in the ultra-competitive car business, every few million dollars mattered.

Previously, Terry's CFO had determined that the Japanese were incurring about 10% assembly costs for the typical module. Since the car companies were using inside labor, the CFO knew that the assembly could be done more cheaply on the outside. The issue was how to control the quality. Terry and his team didn't need to look any farther than the quality control engineers who created and oversaw the program for the car companies. Fortunately, the Japanese had highly similar quality programs, so Terry only needed to hire the team of three engineers from one of the customers. No need to re-create the wheel when these engineers were going to be out of a job anyway. As expected, they were motivated to work with Super Films to make the program successful.

Super Films was a manufacturer, not an assembler. When Terry pitched the car companies, he already had a partnership deal with an assembling company. There are many companies who assemble modules of all types. These companies are highly efficient and cost-effective. Normally they locate their facilities in low-cost areas, so their rates are highly competitive.

Without making any other improvements to the assembly process, Terry believed Super would earn about $2 million per year per module. This figure mainly represented the cost difference between what the Japanese car companies were paying to assemble the modules and what it would cost Super to do it. This return was pure as Super Films had very little cost in the program. The Japanese were carrying the working capital costs of the program, plus the fixtures and equipment used in the assembly process were relatively inexpensive.

But Terry wasn't done saving and making money. He knew that his film could be applied to a wide variety of inexpensive materials. In effect, a Super Films' finish looked great regardless of the substrate material. Terry's materials engineers were experts in identifying and testing various inexpensive materials that would work with their films. The engineers had been busy with the modules, and they were able to take substantial costs out of the module. Terry negotiated a 50/50 sharing with the Japanese on these costs, which added another $1 million per year per module to Super.

MIDAS MOMENT

At the end of the first year, Terry had achieved the following: 1) controlled his space to protect the 38% gross margins on his films; 2) added about $10 million per year to Super Films' earnings; 3) accomplished #1 and #2 with little investment.

Terry considered what Super had accomplished within a fairly short period of time. This assembly program had increased the value of Super Films by tens of millions of dollars. He knew the American car companies would eventually lessen their command-and-control ways and knock on his door, or they would go out of business. Assuming the former happened, Terry thought he might answer and let them in. On second thought …

BLUEPRINT

Companies of all sizes are outsourcing in order to leverage their core competencies. The foregoing story has two examples of outsourcing: first the car company outsources to Super Films; then Super Films outsources the assembly work to a third party. The economy and its players become more efficient as everyone plays to their strengths.

In the Aggregation Age, companies will either aggregate their space, or they will be aggregated. Wealth goes to the former; a living or lifestyle awaits the latter. Terry and Super Films chose to create wealth. This is a decision that every business owner must make. Most choose to bear substantial risk of ownership without receiving the corresponding return. This has always amazed me, perhaps more than anything else I've seen on Main Street. Imagine buying a bond that promises to pay 7% interest, but after six months it becomes clear that the bond will pay only 2%. All business owners would scream if they were the owner of the underperforming bond. Yet most live with this condition every day in their business. Yes, they willingly make this choice.

Companies that aggregate their space successfully will create tremendous value, usually without investing large amounts of capital to support it. This is far different than consolidating companies, which involves tons of cash to acquire companies. Super Films spent less than a few months of incremental cash flow to aggregate its space. It's always a good idea to invest when the payback is this quick.

The following steps can be used to create and implement a modularized strategy:

Become a space integrator

The main way of aggregating your space is to control more of your supply chain. It requires substantial study to determine how best to bundle or modularize the space. But studying is far cheaper than going out and acquiring a bunch of companies.

Package or bundle your value proposition

Typically you can sell the ultimate customer on a pro forma basis, so you don't have to spend the time and money to aggregate until after you receive a green light. Always begin by offering the value proposition to the customer. It's essential that you tune in to WIFM.

Control without owning all of the assets

You should be able to aggregate your space with a minimum of out-of-pocket investment. A well architected plan focuses more on intellectual capital leverage than on financial leverage.

Create a leverage machine

Creating a bundle works for you as the aggregator as long as you leverage your position. It's not enough just to capture more sales; the goal is to add value. The key is creating scalable value architecture so each stakeholder benefits — beginning with you.

It's a paradox that Midas Managers accomplish so much by working so little — or at least they don't work hard in a traditional sense. This is counter-intuitive, and most managers simply can't imagine leveraging themselves so completely that they no longer need to do any tactical work. Here's the secret: until a manager can imagine a life without their fingerprints on the problems, they will likely never achieve financial independence.

MIDAS MOMENT

INVESTMENT BANKER MAN

A mirror: That's where this business owner
needs to look to see the real problem

18

A GLOBAL NICHE-AHOLIC

When Rob Thompson was growing up, he never imagined that he would eventually become the lapel pin king of the world. But he dared to dream, and just a few decades later, he was selling more pins than anyone else. The journey from growing up in a small town in Vermont to doing business in dozens of countries around the world was not an easy one.

HOW TO SURVIVE BY EXPANDING

If timing really is everything, Rob shouldn't still be in business. He was just getting started in the promotional products industry when the terrible recession of 1991 hit. Buying all but stopped in America for the next two years. This was a moment of truth. Rob could either pack it in and find a real job, or double down and bet the ranch. He did the latter, mainly by taking out very expensive ads in national magazines. Basically, he pushed all of his life savings into the ads.

Fortunately, people responded. Rob sent out hundreds of free samples, which converted into dozens of new customers. By 1993, PinSource (PS) was a national company. Before long, it would go global.

The next big push came in the form of advertising in airline magazines. It turns out that corporate executives actually read these things. By advertising every month in each magazine, PinSource attracted hundreds of new customers. Before Rob knew it, Pin-Source was the #1 lapel pin supplier in America.

Executives from around the world fly in airplanes as well. Pin-Source started sending pins to Asia and Europe with increasing frequency. So Rob rolled the dice and exhibited at a major promotional trade show in Germany. The show went so well that PS opened its first office overseas in the Netherlands. It wasn't long afterward that serious learning occurred.

THE 1000 YEAR WAR

It wasn't a mistake opening an office in Amsterdam. The real mistake was bringing in an international staff and thinking that an office in the Netherlands could sell a commodity product throughout Europe. Unbeknown to Rob, the Dutch didn't want to buy from Germans, Germans didn't want to buy from Dutch, and pretty much everyone hated the French. In other words, the cultural wars that had raged across Europe for a millennium were still alive and well. Sure, some tariffs had been eliminated and it was easier to move goods across the countries' borders. In certain cases, however, you just couldn't sell across borders. And Rob had created such a case. By locating in a small country with its own language and culture, Rob was unable to sell successfully outside of the Netherlands.

Rob learned another big lesson early: in Europe, it is nearly impossible to fire someone. His early hire was a bad fit for what PS needed. It's easier in Europe to just hire someone better and create a make-work job for someone than to let them go. So that's what Rob did. Plus, he retreated to a more neutral country — Austria. Austria, it turns out, is a great place to sell into Germany. Germans love the place. Apparently the Von Trapp family singers left a positive, lasting impression on that country.

Even in beautiful Salzburg, Rob noticed that things operate differently than in beautiful Vermont. Behavior was different throughout the system. Decisions were made differently by buyers. The workers' and supply chains' pace was different. This led to Rob's #1 Rule for operating overseas: different cultures operate differently. Respect the differences if you want to be successful. Open-mindedness and the ability to adapt are the keys. After several years of trial-and-error learning, PinSource was solidly positioned in Europe.

WHY NOT THE WORLD?

With his Napoleon-esque conquest of the continent behind him, Rob decided to go directly to Asia. He opened in Hong Kong, which got him closer to major customers, plus solidified his major supply sources in China. And then the global floodgates opened. He launched offices in numerous countries, including Central and South America.

MIDAS MOMENT

Rob standardized his expansion advance. Most importantly, he built around people he knew and trusted. This meant that the opportunity in a particular country was secondary to the manager. PS's model attracted talented people. As Rob became comfortable with them, he would open an office in their country. Together they would form a plan, which leveraged the manager's talents and PS's model.

The critical success factor for PinSource was to attract customers -- once they attracted a prospect, the company's close rate was outstanding. The company acquired leads through the Internet. Now, there is a science to getting noticed on the Net. Most companies use pay-per-click advertising, which for lapel pins costs around $9 per click. This proved to be extremely expensive for a lapel pin supplier, as more than 50% of the clickers had no intention of buying anything. This was costing PinSource more than $35,000 per month! Rob believed there was a better way.

Enter Search Engine Optimization (SEO). This is the process of improving the volume and quality of traffic to a website from search engines via algorithmic search results. Usually, the earlier a site is presented in the search results, or the higher it "ranks," the more searchers will visit that site. Rob spent a ton of time and a fair amount of money on SEO to improve PS's search position. It didn't always work, but it improved the quality and cost-effectiveness of its leads and helped cut costs. Fortunately, lapel pins are used everywhere. So is the Internet. SEO is a worldwide solution.

It seems highly improbable that a company could do millions of dollars a year in sales by selling only lapel pins. It's a highly customized, heavily designed product that requires 8-10 emails before final delivery. The average order is less than $1,000. It is not a consumable; PinSource's lapel pins last many years. So how does PS do it?

Rob says he is a global niche-aholic. PinSource just does lapel pins better than any other company in the world. No single country buys enough pins to meet Rob's sales goals. But there are a lot of lapels walking around in the world. By doing one thing extremely well, PS can dominate its space. It just shows that no matter where you start in life, the world is the only boundary that really matters.

MIDAS MOMENT

BLUEPRINT

In real life, Rob Thompson is Rob Rothman. His company is SUI Brands. He is from Vermont, and he really is a global niche-aholic.

Most Midas Managers in private companies are niche-aholics. In the Aggregation Age we are seeing the emergence of global niches. America needs more owners to make markets overseas. As it stands now, a very small percentage of middle market companies achieve even 25% of their annual sales through foreign sales. This needs to change.

Globalization has dramatically affected the size of niches. During the 1980s, a middle market company could develop, and defend, a niche with $50 million per year in sales. Then, in the 1990s, the sandbox got bigger and the size of niches fell in half, to about $25 million. This halving has happened again in the current decade. Today, if a mid-sized company gets much above $10 million in sales from a niche, the world shows up, and they're not looking to buy.

This is why most successful domestic middle market companies are really amalgams of niches hanging from an intellectual capital tree. We might call these companies niched conglomerates. Successful companies often operate in six to eight niches, each with less than $10 million in sales but tremendous overall profitability. For Midas Managers, it's not about total sales; it's about how much wealth is created — now and in the future.

Successful global middle market companies, like the one examined in this chapter, may exploit just one niche worldwide. Let's agree on something: if you can build a medium-sized company by selling only lapel pins worldwide, you can do it with just about any product or service. There's a big advantage to focusing on a single value proposition and refining it to the point of competitive advantage. We might refer to this as niche value architecture.

The following steps can be used to replicate a global niching strategy:

Become a niche-aholic in your own country

You need to become niche-centric domestically before you start picking foreign fights. There are certain attributes that niche-ahol-ism requires, such as knowledge of behavior in a space, a tight value proposition, and solid customer leads. These must be built before they can be exported.

Pick your partner first

People and talent trump a country. Choose your partner and key managers carefully. Then let them guide you in the customs and culture of doing business in the new country. Be aware that some parts of your domestic model will not work in every country — so be flexible.

MIDAS MOMENT

Leverage the machine

Quickly determine what parts of your marketing machine work in the particular country, then leverage that plus your partner's talents. Obviously, customer attraction is the most important part of the machine — so focus on that first.

Don't be afraid to add more niches

Usually you'll be able to add niches once you're established in a country. For instance, the company profiled in this chapter has successfully added complimentary promotional products to its offerings. Ultimately, the goal is to hang several niches off the intellectual capital tree in each country.

I think we all need to become black hole niche-aholics in our respective fields. Once we maximize our domestic space, we should evolve into global niche-aholism. A future book — *Midas Micro Multinationals* — will show how Midas Managers make markets in countries around the world. Many of the marketing activities are the same, regardless of country: generating leads; converting these leads into customers; servicing the customers in a value-added way. But there are substantial differences when it comes to selling in foreign countries. Different cultures require different treatment. This requires picking your partners with special care, plus adapting to the circumstances. But global riches wait for those who exploit global niches.

19

CREATING A VIRTUOUS CYCLE

Author's Note: If you've made it this far into the book, or read my other books, you've gathered that I believe most business owners are not competing well in the global economy. Many aren't competing at all; others can't find the resources to help them. In any event, the majority of the U.S. economy is generated by private companies, and it's beyond time that business owners got into the value creation game. This final story describes what I'm doing to improve this situation in America.

A couple of years ago I had an "Aha!" moment — a flash of clarity that has sustained me to the present. In that instant, I realized there was a way to solve a handful of seemingly intractable problems in one fell swoop. The problems: universities across America were not teaching students how to become successful business owners; young business owners could not find mentors to help them get to the next level; and successful ex-business owners did not have a platform to help either students or younger business owners meet their goals. The solution to this trifecta of problems: Midas Institutes. But I need to take you back in time for you to fully see how this idea germinated.

THREE YEARS PRIOR

I opened a rather large box one day, and staring at me was a geodesic dome sitting on top of a five-pound book with the words "Private Capital Markets" (PCMs) printed boldly on the front. Here was proof that four years of constant work could be tangibly represented. For a minute, I once again considered how unjustifiable it was to spend 6,000 hours writing a textbook that had no course it could support, no university that even knew it existed, and no following — even among practitioners. I was caught somewhere between pride of authorship and a feeling of total idiocy.

I hadn't expected to spend four years writing PCMs. I thought I could complete it in 18 months. Here's a lesson for all aspiring authors: don't tell a soul that you're writing a book, for if you do, you'll need to finish it even when you realize just how big an undertaking it really is. But I had made the mistake of spilling the beans. I'd already told a mainly disinterested world that I was attempting to create a new field of study called Private Finance. And my vehicle was this textbook.

If you have any sense at all, you'll never write a textbook. The main problem is audience-related. Unless you already have standing as an academic, the chances of getting a new course adopted around the book are the kind of odds you face in a state lottery. I was foremost a practitioner, with a healthy disdain for most things academic. I didn't reach this position haphazardly. I received far more education than my parents and family thought was necessary. Along the way, I witnessed what happens to people when they teach about subjects they have not personally experienced. This is the equivalent of gladiators giving fighting lessons when they've never entered the arena. And this is how I viewed (and still view) most business academics.

So, with this unhealthy attitude, I started knocking on university doors to see if anyone would offer the new semester-long course I had created (also called Private Capital Markets). This is when I discovered something else about mainstream business academia: they really only want to study and teach public company stuff. It's as if the only job that exists in their world is middle manager of a large public company. I started to get the feeling that most business academics were trapped, by their own choosing, in 1975. This was the era when U.S. multinationals ruled the world, and every business student needed to be aimed in their direction. Somehow, academia had missed the last few decades, in which Main Street had overtaken Wall Street relative to career paths and most other meaningful metrics.

MIDAS MOMENT

THE BREAKTHROUGH

After a couple of years of harping, we finally got the course approved at Suffolk University in Boston. Thank you, Shariar Khaksari and John Leonetti, for your yeomen job of getting the course approved and then teaching it so expertly. This also made it possible to teach the course at other schools. While it was still a tough political battle to get the course adopted, at least we could say it was being taught.

It was easy to notice that virtually no business owners were reading PCMs. It turns out that most business owners didn't read textbooks while they were going to school, so the chances of them reading a textbook 20 years later were nil. Most owners had stopped reading all business books many years before, as they were smart enough to know that the Jack Welches of the world had nothing to say to them. Business owners simply can't see how to apply most business books' Wall Street ideas to their small companies (neither can I, by the way). So I wrote *Midas Managers* for owners and their advisors. *Midas Managers* illustrates how to apply the theories and constructs developed in PCMs. Since *Midas* is mainly a story book, owners, for once, actually read and enjoyed a business book.

The problem is getting even a relevant book into private business owners' hands. They don't exactly spend their off-hours browsing at Barnes & Noble. You nearly need to hit an owner upside his head (women are more amenable to reading) to get them to read a business book. I needed help.

In Midasville, when in doubt, change the rules. I created a new class of advisor — called Midas Advisors — to help break through to the business owner community. I co-branded the book with CPAs, lawyers, financial planners, money managers and other professionals. Each Midas Advisor bought fairly large quantities of copies of *Midas Managers* for further distribution. Their name was on the cover of *Midas Managers* with mine; their bio and picture was next to mine on the inside flap of the dust jacket. In effect, *Midas Managers* became their new business cards. This explains how *Midas Managers* was a top selling private business book the year it came out. And not a single copy was sold through a bookstore.

It wasn't enough just to co-brand the book, however. I also needed to empower Midas Advisors to engage their business owner clients in a value-added way. First, I helped the Advisors create their own Wealth Maps. These documents describe how the Advisors can re-conceptualize their role and business model in order to get to Midasville (financial independence). We then started running webcasts that drilled into various Midas strategies and the Midas way of reconceptualizing all businesses. Prospects and clients were invited to these webcasts. We began doing four or five live events each month around the country. These "In Search of the Midas Touch" events ultimately evolved into religious revivals, where the religion is American competitiveness. This is when the "Aha" moment hit me.

MIDAS MOMENT

MIDASNATION

We had created a nation of users. They were in all 50 states, and they were looking for answers to the questions: How can I help America do better?; and How can I become financially independent? And we had answers.

Even with a great cause, we still lacked a unifying structure. Enter the universities. Who could have guessed that my pounding on academic doors the prior few years would now pay off? Many universities had added Entrepreneurial Centers and Incubators which were designed to commercialize technology as well as help people get into business. But the schools lack the organization to help people already in business grow the value of their businesses. Fortunately, the universities have the resources in the form of successful alumni. Many of these alumni have owned numerous businesses, but have ultimately exited them, played a bunch of golf, traveled the world, and are now looking for something to do. Essentially, these Midas Managers are looking for their next challenge. Many want to help the next generation of owners become more successful. We call the Midas Managers who want to coach "Midas Mentors." Chapter 11 in *Midas Managers* describes the outlook and activities of a typical Midas Mentor.

These ideas launched the Midas Institute program. The mission of the Midas Institute initiative is to make American business more competitive going forward by teaching students to become successful business owners; to mentor current business owners ("Mentorees") to their wealth creation goals; and to engage highly successful past business owners ("Mentors") who will mentor the students and Mentorees. Midas Advisors provide ancillary services to the stakeholders. The primary goal is to create a virtuous cycle of success.

Now a large infrastructure has been created to support the Midas Institutes. The www.MidasNation.com site contains substantial content including videos, webcasts, and numerous papers and articles. A number of universities now sponsor an Institute on their campus. Entire alumni networks have been approached to support their "Chapter." In other words, this is one major affinity program.

Let's review the value propositions to each stakeholder group:

Students: They have the opportunity to take the Private Capital Markets (PCMs) course. Each class is taught in three parts. The first third of the class uses the PCMs textbook, which contains theories and structure that describe the behavior of the private markets. The second third of the class employs a student-led case presentation and discussion. Each case study is a modified chapter from the Midas series. The case describes the real world application of the structure learned in the first part. The class ends with a practitioner explaining what it means to do their particular job (e.g., mezzanine capital provider, investment banker, etc.); how to access the career;

MIDAS MOMENT

what the lifestyle and compensation looks like; and what it takes to succeed. Students who can't take the live course can access videos of the course materials.

Students who successfully take either the video or live course are eligible to intern in the program. Thus they get paid for helping where they can; mostly they get paid for learning about business and life from Midas Mentors.

Mentorees: Business owners who have potential and a desire to substantially increase the value of their businesses can access the Program. They begin by engaging the Institute to complete a Company Wealth Map. This is a Map to Midasville, i.e., a roadmap that shows where they are now, and how to get their business to where they want to go. A Midas Mentor oversees the creation of the Map. Basically, the Mentor answers one key question: If the Mentor owned the business and wanted to increase the value of the company five-fold (for example), how would he or she do it? Each Mentor can quickly access the minds of thousands of other Mentors in the system to solve nearly any problem.

For many Mentorees, the general sense of community and achievement they experience is actually more important than the business mentoring. is. At last, they are no longer alone in their quest.

Mentors: Midas Mentors have already achieved financial independence. They have already owned one or more businesses. They've already lived on the other side of the wall, so to speak. But they want to give back. They have an unyielding desire to both see America do better, and help younger owners and students live their dreams. Most of the Mentors are alumni of the university that sponsors a particular Institute, so they get the satisfaction of giving back to their school as well. The Institute is a platform that enables the Mentors to meet these goals.

University: The Midas Institute fills a hole at the university. Many schools now have an incubator or entrepreneurial program, but nothing for middle-market companies. Enter the Institute. The program helps its students and alumni in highly value-added ways. This is done both academically and experientially. Plus, the Institute re-engages many of the school's most successful alumni, and challenges them in a very compelling program.

Midas Advisors: Midas Advisors do almost all of the tactical work for the Chapter. These are the accountants, planners, consultants, money managers, lawyers, and others who have expertise in areas that support the overall program. Advisors benefit by "plugging in" to a steady source of business, in a trusted environment.

MIDAS MOMENT

The Midas Institute program leverages many of the concepts described in this book. The Institute offers compelling value propositions to all stakeholders. Most importantly, MidasNation is making a huge difference in America's ongoing effort to better compete in a global economy. Thus its tagline: "Building America One Business at a Time."

INVESTMENT BANKER MAN

Madison Avenue decides to focus on marketing
rather than advertising

20

THE BIG FINISH

very so often, the Earth's magnetic poles switch: the North Pole becomes South and the South Pole becomes North. Go figure. Many scientists believe the Earth is about to undergo such a geomagnetic reversal in the next thousand years or so. You can just imagine what will happen at O'Hare airport the day after the shift. Surprisingly, the same kind of cataclysmic changes occur in the business world as well, although much more frequently. We call these periods business "Ages." Almost all of the rules of business change in a new Age.

The world entered the Conceptual Age in 2001. On September 11, 2001, the United States was thrust into a global war with terrorists. At about the same time, China entered the World Trade Organization. The combination of these events birthed the Conceptual Age and thrust U.S. businesses into a global war of their own. The Conceptual Age marked the intersection of globalization, logistics, and advanced technology. This Age has been defined by multi-dimensional thinking. It requires business owners to conceptualize their way to success. Operational excellence is no longer enough; in the Conceptual Age, it is merely the starting point. Machines, capital and employees are no longer the main factors in creating business wealth. In the Conceptual Age, the biggest is the manager's ability to conceptualize solutions.

Before the calendar turns to 2010, we will enter the Aggregation Age. Many of us have already warped out of the Conceptual Age and have adopted strategies that aggregate our spaces. This next Age will be characterized by exponential change; by right-brain thinking; by global competition; by advanced leverage of intellectual capital; and by companies that control — not own — their business spaces. The Aggregation Age is the Conceptual Age on steroids.

Abandon hope all ye who ignore the rules of wealth creation of their Age. Let's reconsider some of the Newest Rules of the Aggregation Age:

- Managers must design and implement compelling value propositions for all stakeholders of the firm.

- Value propositions should be packaged and positioned in the crowd, customer base, and supply chain.

- Companies should adopt Pull business models to create value. Further, a company should control — not own — its business space.

- Managers should quality control manage their space chains, i.e., keep their fingers on many pulses, but not leave their fingerprints on the space chain or business.

- Managers should become value architects, and thereby leverage their firm's intellectual capital by at least 10:1.

Play well by the Newest Rules, throw in a few black hole niches, and that's all you need to do. Gee, and you thought it would be difficult to achieve financial independence. All kidding aside, massive wealth is created by early adopters and by those who play especially well by the new rules of their Age. Look at what Bill Gates did in the Information age, or what the Google guys accomplished in the Conceptual Age. Just think what you can do in the Aggregation Age.

MIDAS MOMENT

VALUE PROPOSITIONS REPRISED

Too often, business writers tend to over-complicate the concept of value propositions. This is unfortunate, since everyone in business is a bad value proposition away from oblivion. Value propositions answer one simple question: what's in it for me (WIFM)? As a business owner or manager, it is your primary task to design compelling answers to WIFM. Capitalism demands it. You need to answer the WIFM question successfully to all stakeholders of your firm. But don't forget the most important stakeholder — you! This leads to the more descriptive acronym: WIFUM (what's in it for you and me). Of course, you need to create value as you are implementing compelling value propositions for everyone else.

Chapter 19 gives a real-life example of WIFUM in action. I'm one of those people who is missing a key gene: I can't stop myself from picking fights I obviously can't win. Thus was born the MidasNation initiative. Imagine trying to reconceptualize all of American private business through colleges and universities. That's what we're doing. Now. I like to tell people that when I achieve this modest mission, I'm going after that pesky world hunger problem.

The Midas initiative is designed with each stakeholder in mind. I am doing my best to answer WIFM for each stakeholder group. Now we're executing the aggregation model. My personal goal is to create a virtuous cycle that outlasts me by at least 100 years (that's what's in it for me).

Just designing compelling value propositions isn't enough. You must then package them, or you will become the constraint on your own system. Once again, let's consider the structure of MidasNation. Each university Chapter is basically self-sufficient, but can access all of the other Chapters if it needs help. Each Chapter has a manager who oversees that business. All of the stakeholders have a place on the community website (www.MidasNation.com). Everyone knows what's in it for them and what they are required to do to add value to the system. Once launched, all of this happens without me. I started it, and I attracted resources into it, but I can't be in the middle of it, or it will not meet its full potential. I've had to check my control freak nature at the MidasNation door. Somewhat paradoxically, the less I put my hands on the program going forward, the better it will do.

THE PULL IS THE FORCE

We've all been trained to push ... push ... push in life. This orientation worked in a slow-changing world, where operating leverage was low. But now the world is changing exponentially, and pushing is not an effective force. This is just one reason why most salespeople — the ultimate pushing force — will not do well in the Aggregation Age. But pulling is efficient in this Age. The Internet provides the perfect Pull environment.

MIDAS MOMENT

All of the stories in this book involve pulling the crowd, customer or space to the Midas Managers' company. What a plethora of opportunities! Think about it. There are three main groups to pull, and probably hundreds of strategies by which to accomplish it. The only thing stopping you is you.

Crowdsourcing is the most important concept to hit my mind in many years. I was hooked the minute I read that Proctor & Gamble had used the crowd to solve a major operating issue with Crest toothpaste. You should be hooked as well. The world has substantial open capacity — all you need to do is ask for help (and maybe kick in a few bucks). The first four story chapters show you how to do it. Get busy pulling the crowd.

Most owner-managers will focus on pulling the customer. There's nothing wrong with this. The power of attraction is critical here. The main reason people buy in a capitalistic society is because they believe the purchase is value-added to them. It's your job to make sure prospective customers know about your value proposition, and that you provide an easy way for them to grab the hook — repeatedly. The fishing metaphor is particularly useful here. First you need to select the appropriate bait (value proposition). Then you need to determine where the fish might be (study the market). Then you need to cast your line (push the first time). Then you pull in the fish (using a net whenever possible).

Aggregating your space may be the most fun way to pull. These tend to be "big bang for the bucks" strategies. These typically do not add incremental sales; rather, aggregating a space usually results in major sales moves. Chapter 17 shows how I was able to reorient one business into a space integrator, as opposed to a one-off parts supplier. It cost little money to implement this strategy, but the results were phenomenal. I'm convinced that managers in most spaces can successfully copy this strategy.

MANAGERS AS VALUE ARCHITECTS

Midas Managers are a rare breed: perhaps only 1 in 1,000 business owners reach this status. Some cataclysm in life empowers some people to become fearless, which may lead to Midas management. But it's impossible to predict who will become a Midas Manager.

Fortunately, anyone can become a value architect. This is perhaps the single most important thing I have learned since authoring *Midas Managers*. What does it mean to be a value architect? It means you spend most of your time designing and implementing vigorous value propositions for your stakeholders. It means you have selected and are implementing Pull marketing strategies in an Aggregation business model. It means that you have your fingers on the pulse, but no fingerprints on your business. It means you can take three or four months off each year without detriment to

MIDAS MOMENT

your business. It means that you're either financially independent already, or that you're on the right path to this conclusion.

Most business owners are not value architects; rather, they are either tradespeople (e.g., carpenters) or general contractors to their businesses. The former group generates a living; the latter generates a lifestyle. Neither is likely to realize financial independence. My goal for this book is to help convert more owners to value architects. As with most really important things, this conversion is more about behavioral change than spending money to achieve it. You've got to truly want to become a value architect to become one.

THE REALLY BIG FINISH

I've learned so much writing this book. I didn't realize the importance of marketing until I started owning businesses. I used to think that commerce starts with a sale. Now I know better. It starts with good marketing — which then causes a sale. Hopefully, this book has convinced you of the importance of marketing to your business' future success.

I've also recently learned that there are three kinds of people. The first group sees the glass as half-full, because that's the way they want to see the world. The second group sees the glass as half-empty, because that's how they see the world. The third group includes Midas Managers. They just see liquid in a glass. If they need to fill or empty the glass, they will select appropriate strategies and tactics to get the job done. This dispassionate view of their environment is one of their core strengths. While we all need faith that things will ultimately work out, Midas Managers remind us that hope is not an effective strategy.

In the Aggregation Age, companies that leverage their intellectual capital the most will win. Those companies that pull the crowd, customer, and aggregate their space will create tremendous value; those companies that don't do these things will be hard pressed to survive. Companies with a goal of incremental improvement are in big trouble. Success will go to the revolutionaries; to those that achieve geometric results. The incrementalists who seek 5-10% annual improvement are effectively dead already.

We have a major economic problem in America: we're not creating enough value on Main Street. The majority of America's economy is generated by private businesses — not Wall Street. More than 80% of new jobs are created by private companies. Yet, the vast majority of private business owners are not increasing the value of their firms. In other words, most owners are not practicing what's in this book. This is a major threat to the continued sovereignty of the United States.

MIDAS MOMENT

I'm old-fashioned in how I view the American dream. For me, it's not about accumulating expensive homes, cars and toys. I believe the American dream represents the opportunity and obligation of one generation to leave this country better off for the next generation. The Boomer generation has failed in this mission. This is not acceptable.

The Preface of this book quotes Einstein: "If at first the idea is not absurd, then there is no hope for it." My absurd idea is that I can help millions of owners and managers compete better in a global economy. And in so doing, help my generation meet its most important obligation to our kids.

MIDAS MOMENT

MIDAS MOMENT

MIDAS MOMENT

MIDAS MOMENT

MIDAS MOMENT